ABOUT THE AUTHOR

Ngozi "Angie" Okoko was born in Lagos, Nigeria and raised in the Eastern part of Imo state, save for her relocation to Lagos, where she completed her primary education. She went on to move to the United Kingdom, where she studied Business with Accounting and Finance at the University of the West of England, Bristol. *Ngozichukwu: A Memoir of Grace*, is her debut novel, which comes after a long, arduous journey of finding her way.

She is the wife of an engineer and sibling to four gems, who also live in the UK. When she isn't being a financial controller, Ngozi is a serial entrepreneur involved in the food and fashion industries. Other times, she's a philomath with a degree spread capable of awing the unimpressionable: MBA, CMgr, BA (Hons), MA, DipFS, MCMI, CIMA, PhD (in view).

Ngozi is a people person and a great storyteller with a penchant for luring readers into her world of hope, where God is alive, everyone is free to be whomever or whatever they please, the air smells nice, and the foods are healthy.

Page intentionally left blank

NGOZICHUKWU

A Memoir of Grace

By Ngozi Okoko

ngozibello21@gmail.com

Gloucester, UK 07496509251

Page intentionally left blank

Cover design by **Designer Abrefa**

V1.0_ur

Page intentionally left blank

ACKNOWLEDGEMENT

My sincerest thanks to everyone who has hurt, hated, or treated me unfairly, without whom I'd not now be where I am. It's the corniest thing to give a shout-out to haters, but it's a fact that I'm stronger, better, and in a much grander place because they made me feel uncomfortable enough to want more. I've always believed that people help and hurt me for a reason: to teach me to aspire or stay.

But I can't get carried away with the villains of my story and forget to thank the true heroes/heroines that saved the day one too many times. To my mom and superwoman, I bless God for your life and his hand upon you. For a single mother, you are proof that parenting can be done right.

To my grandmother—the strongest woman that paved the way for me—nnoo! You raised me as your own and taught me to be the strong woman that I've grown to be.

To my darling husband, you have my love. Thank you for standing by me and being a place of solace in troubling times. Thank you for believing in me and in this writing. You've been an inspiration!

To irreplaceable siblings who taught me what family could be, I love you all.

And lastly, to friends, who became family along the way, even those I couldn't mention in this book—you all complete my story.

Page intentionally left blank

CONTENTS

Page intentionally left blank

PREFACE

Writing this book was my most challenging task yet because it involves a whole range of bittersweet memories, including ones that still keep me awake at night, and the ones that bring a smile to my face. This is my little way of putting my story out there to encourage everyone who's had or is having it rough. It might seem like much now, and the future may look blurry, but like everything else, fates change. It could happen in a snap, a day, a week, a month, a year, you name it. As long as you're willing to keep believing in yourself and be courageous enough to keep pushing, you'll overcome the trials of life.

Remember that life is one long battle. And the only time you lose is when you give up. If you keep going, you just might win.

Beyond the courage to tell my difficult tale, I also had to deal with reliving the emotions of memories I'd rather forget. Tears have splattered across my notes and devices from the many times I've tried to brave it. But it'd all have been worth it if it teaches the fearful to find courage, helps the weak find strength, helps the uninspired find inspiration, and teaches the lackadaisical to never give up. You see, life hangs on the swing of time and chance. It could be your big break today or your undoing the next.

Also, you shouldn't look down on anyone—not even yourself. No one is without their share of inabilities or incompetence, and that isn't nearly enough reason to dismiss them. Never in a million years did I picture myself having a remarkable career and life. I grew up knowing something was wrong with me, even though people did their best to pretend that they weren't the ones pointing it out. I knew I was an underdog with my disabilities and had heard it severally from people who turned me down. In the end, everything works together for good.

I want to thank everyone who's taken the time to read my story. Now, you share a part of me that's helped me grow to my present state and are more enlightened on the journey to whatever you now make of me. Your support from the purchase is acknowledged, and I hope you get your own happy moments, like the little victories that helped me survive the yesteryears.

Page intentionally left blank

"Eagles fly when lesser birds cannot fly. So, eagles can do what lesser birds cannot do." —T. D. Jakes

1

BORN DIFFERENT

I was five when I discovered how different I was from my peers. Not only were their legs straighter, but they also spoke clearly and without the lisp I heard in my pronunciations. I was born as a sickly child, and my mom was advised to do away with me. According to the "experts," my chances of survival were next to nothing. My grandparents and mom fought for my survival, with the former insisting on taking me in to prevent anyone convincing my mom otherwise.

With their limited exposure and education, they took me everywhere that promised a cure, however far-fetched it might seem. According to my grandfather, I was the most unresponsive child he'd ever held. I neither suckled nor moved. My mom shared similar sentiments. If I was left on a spot, I was rooted there until someone moved me again. When they could help it, I had a bit of formula.

Their persistence for a miracle paid off in the end when they met a woman called Ann. Besides the laundry list of abnormal symptoms I presented, I also had hair sticking out of my skin like some weird ape-human hybrid. Auntie Ann, as I'd grow to call the woman that saved my life, found an herbal remedy that I was placed on for several months. At the end of the medication, I achieved a significant degree of normalcy.

But there were some trade-offs for my determination to live. I grew up with a bad case of bandy-leggedness that made Nne, my grandmother, tie my legs during bedtime. She made me lie flat on the bed and put my legs together, holding them in place with pieces torn from an old wrapper. Nne believed it'd help my legs straighten out. I was none the wiser, so I let her.

Waking up each day to the pain of walking and ignoring it for so long my brain failed to process it was normal for me. It didn't help that my grandparents, my primary guardians, weren't well off and neither were their children. In fact, my uncles and aunts could barely manage their own families, let alone have enough to help out their aged forebears. For sustenance, we relied heavily on the produce from my grandfather's farm. As a result, I grew into the life of farming for food.

I'd return from school and head for jakpa farm—one of Mpa's farmland that was furthest away from where we lived. There, I planted and harvested cassava for our meals and earnings. For the day's meal, if Nne wasn't already onto something, I returned home with the harvests and decided between making abacha[1] and garri[2].

For the latter, since it was more intensive and produced more end products, I took any excess to the evening market to make the family some money. If the garri was ready before I left for school, I took it to Nne's shed at the local market. After school hours, I headed for the market to help sell out whatever remained of the load.

During the weekends and holidays, I spent my time peddling groundnuts across the village. When things got dire, like when I had to pay certain bills at school, I went as far as peddling okpa[3] before school started for the day. I also learned to make palm oil at an early age. When Mpa's palm nuts weren't in season, I gathered fallen bits from other farmlands until I had enough to milk their precious juice. The resulting palm oil went into my petty

---

[1] A local snack made from cassava (also, African salad)
[2] Cassava flakes
[3] Bambara groundnut

trades, with a little portion left behind for in-house cooking.

Ukwa[4] didn't escape my sight either. I gathered, sun-dried, and sold them whenever I could. Basically, if it could be eaten and had some trading value, I sold it.

Keeping up such a demanding routine meant that I couldn't afford to nap. While my peers fell asleep with full bellies and woke up to dinner, I spent my afternoons slaving to get food and money.

Another item on my itinerary was local oil lamps, which I made and sold. Like everything else, I kept some for myself, which I used for going snail hunting with my friends. When the seasons were right, I grew mushrooms and sold udara[5].

You'd think I got several grand gestures for all my troubles. But neither my grandparents nor my aunts and uncles had enough to even get me a change of clothes. So, I repeated my wears until they were worn out from continuous washing and wearing. However, what I couldn't get from home, I got from others in recognition.

The dexterity of trading anything and everything earned me the praise of the villagers, who

---

[4] Breadfruit porridge
[5] African star apple

were quick to nickname me agu nwanyi[6]. For them, it was commendable what I was doing. But for me, it was just another Tuesday.

My life was a cycle of toiling from dawn to dusk. I woke up by 4 a.m., starting off my activities by sweeping the compound and heating any remnants of the previous night's meal. Breakfast in my grandparents' household was the leftovers, which ranged from abacha to fufu[7] to garri to yam. Anything else was a luxury we couldn't afford, rice, beans, eggs, chicken, and bread especially.

Jesus could've visited and we'd have offered him fufu.

In fact, when some relatives that visited from the city brought us bread, Nne hid it away. It was slightly mouldy the next time we had it, but I couldn't dare to complain.

Our diet was so fufu-centric that every meal we had in the day was the same as the previous one. If we switched it up, we just went back to another food we already had sometime within the week: yam, garri, or abacha. It didn't help that I didn't like yam; so that was another food off my already restricted diet.

---

[6] Lioness
[7] Soft, doughy staple

The food was also plain the bulk of the time, save some Mangala fish that Nne ground or broke into the soup. Beef and kanda[8] were foods I imagined or saw on the plates of other people.

The Cycle of Life

Regardless of our poor background, Nne was quite the disciplinarian. She handled me firmly and never spared the rod when I erred. At the time, I felt slighted at how she descended on me every other time. But in retrospect, she was correcting me the only way she saw fit.

When Nne wasn't beating the devil out of me, we had great moments and I was very helpful. I'd take her clothes to the stream to wash and swam in the water while waiting for them to dry. My life was as straightforward as it was arduous, but it was all I knew and was used to. I couldn't even afford to be sick. Not because there were no local treatments, but because we didn't have nearly enough to cater for one who *might not make it*.

Once, I was bitten by a dog. Like living with bandy legs and being poor wasn't enough punishment already. I was taken to an herbalist who

---

[8] Cow hide

gave us some ointments and herbal drinks. It's a miracle how I survived that.

In contrast, Mpa loved me to death. He was the calm-headed one of my grandparents and spoiled me to his limits. He didn't have much to give but gave the little he had almost always. Since he couldn't afford luxurious items, he fed me from his own food and allowed me to feast on his leftovers, some of which he intentionally left on the plate.

To my grandfather, I was Peppe, due to my hot-headedness. I returned every insult passed at me with equal temerity, if not more. Sometimes, this trait earned me his cane, other times, he praised me.

One time, I was on the way home with my friends, going on about the day at school and how much fun we'd had when along came the devil. This random woman, who was either too stupid to mind her business or too reckless to control her utterances, commented on my cleft palate.

"Ọbụna dịka o siiri gị ike ikwu okwu, ị gbachi nkịtị,"[9] she scoffed, clicking her tongue.

The conversation between my friends died out immediately. I turned to catch her gaze, wagging a finger at her.

----

[9] "Even with your condition, you sure are a talkative."

"Ebe ọ bụ na ị gaghị eche maka azụmahịa gị, ụmụ gị na ụmụ ụmụ gị ga-ekwu ihe a."[10]

The woman was old enough to be my mother, but even she was taken aback by the ferocity and speed I retorted with. She made another snide comment as she went on her way, albeit quietly this time.

"Peppe!" my friends teased, pushing my head playfully. "Agu nwanyi!"

I bit back a smile, happy at my latest victory.

The incident was pretty much forgotten to me until the busybody lady showed up at Mpa's house the next day. I overheard my grandfather conversing with someone in the yard but was too busy with responsibilities to check out the visitor.

"Peppe!" Mpa's voice croaked through the house.

"Mpa'm!" I replied, straining as I rose from an upturned mortar from which I was peeling some freshly harvested cassava.

No sooner had I made it to the front yard than someone fell to their knees before me.

---

[10] "Since you can't mind your business, your children and grandchildren will speak this way."

8

"Biko gbaghara m!"[11]

It took me a moment to identify the face, talk less of making out the connection to the incident. Frankly, I hadn't taken my words for anything beyond the defensive banter I'd grown accustomed to as protection against bullying. So, seeing a grown woman on her knees was quite the spectacle.

But Mpa had taught me too well to be disrespectful or look down on people in vulnerable situations. I forgave her and returned to my work. Mpa beamed at how I'd managed the situation, a sense of pride evident in how he dismissed the woman.

I was close to my grandfather for many reasons, but chief of which was the fact that I reminded him of his mother. According to him, the large birthmark running across the side of my neck was synonymous with the one his mother sustained on return from war. To him, I was a reincarnation of my great-grandmother.

Overstretched as it sounded, the villagers shared his sentiments. Before I knew my speech condition was called cleft palate, the local folks termed me a special child.

If only!

---

[11] "Please, forgive me!"

***

Regardless of my stringent relationship with Nne, I didn't hold anything against her. She was doing her best in a bad situation and I had to try to be as little trouble as possible. But I was still a child and my heart was brimming with folly.

One quality that annoyed her the most was keeping late nights. Not that I was in the habit of staying out, but sometimes, I just forgot the time or overplayed to notice it was nightfall. At such moments when I'd return all sweaty and panting from my run back home, Nne would chide me about the risk of early pregnancy and how I became more susceptible to it the longer I stayed outside.

Yeah, right! Bandy-leggedness and cleft palate—quite the milkshakes that brought the boys to the yard.

No matter how hard I pretended that it wasn't getting to me, I wound up crying my eyes out. But I couldn't hate Nne. She was the only mother I knew. Had she not refused to give up on me?

A mother's love for her child is infinite, innit?

Once, living expenses ran high and all our petty jobs combined could not keep us afloat. Mpa's farms were performing poorly, so there wasn't much for Nne and me to sell. Other wares I peddled had

10

plummeted in value due to the oversaturation of seasonal markets. When things didn't start to look up, I was sent to live with a relative, an aunt, who was receptive for the first few days. But as the days rolled by, she grew into a manipulative, maltreating psychopath.

I knew it was up to me to save myself, so I upped and left one day, returning to my grandparents' house.

2

MOM

I heard I was born in the thriving and overpopulated city of Lagos. I say "heard" because the farthest memories of myself blur into the tiny body of a petite, underfed child stuck in a campestral area of Okohia, Isiekenesi, Ideato South, Imo state. Life, for me, didn't begin until I was eight. Before then, I remember little of who I was and how I'd lived: disabled, overworked, and poor. But that year would go on to mark the beginning of memories to come: happy and sad ones alike.

It was one of those days when life was uneventful, and time seemed to drag its feet. Save the chirpings of insects and the call of birds and chickens roosting in the shadows, all was lull.

It was a market day and everyone with anything to buy or sell was at the village square, haggling and showing off goods beneath the fiery glare of the sun. It would be evening before the village rang with the hustle and bustle of its inhabitants again. Mpa[12], my grandfather, had gone to the village square himself to sell off the extra bits of bushmeat his traps had caught, leaving me at home with Nne[13], my grandmother.

While Nne laboured over a tray of melon seeds, breaking off the outer coating in preparation for the evening meal, I squatted over dirty dishes in the usekwu[14], turning over some freshly washed cookware. I rose briefly to collect myself, stretching to get some feeling back into my waist. Beads of sweat collected across my forehead, running down my face in tiny rivulets. I yawned wildly, slightly catching Nne's voice calling to me.

---

[12] Father
[13] Mother
[14] Kitchen, typically detached from the main house.

"Peppe!"

I stiffened, cocking my head to listen.

Quiet.

What did the villagers say about bad spirits calling to little children again?

Already shrugging off the slight sense of fear that was starting to creep in, I heard Nne's voice again, louder this time, unmistakable too.

"Peppe!"

"Nne," I screamed back, rinsing my hands and running into the house. I raced past the store and room I shared with my grandmother, towards the obi[15], where I found her in the company of a woman with two kids.

"Ndewo nu,"[16] I curtseyed to the visitor before turning to my grandmother, who was all smiles and mute like a child struggling to keep a secret.

I eyed the visitor from the corner of my eyes, entranced by her splendour and grace. She looked and smelled expensive, standing out against the bleak interior of my grandfather's mud cum blockhouse.

---

[15] Detached area occupied by the family head
[16] "Good day."

Ndi oyibo pepper,[17] I thought to myself.

The children looked well off, as well, with more cheeks on their faces than there was flesh on my bones. They looked younger and radiated a similar glow to the woman. I figured they were her kids.

"Peppe," Nne finally dared to speak. "Lee nne gị."[18]

The words rang in my ears before I could even make sense of it. I turned away from my grandmother, glancing from the visitor to her children.

If this is my mother, it means those kids are my siblings. Yeah, right.

"Nne hapụ m biko[19]," I returned my gaze to my grandmother, brows furrowed in confusion. "I no believe you."

Nne laughed raucously, throwing back her head. My supposed mother smiled warmly. The kids just stared, too young to understand or too disinterested to care.

---

[17] White people, in this case, referencing skin tone.
[18] "Look at your mother."
[19] "Nne, let me be." (Implying, *Stop pulling my legs*)

I studied the visitor long and hard, trying to make sense of the sudden discovery. The woman had the skin of a foreigner and a face too shapely to be compared to mine. I'd studied my reflection in Mpa's mirror only too well to see any sort of semblance. I had little memories of my mother; with all I knew of her coming from Mpa's stories. Apparently, my mother forsook her life in the city to nurse me to health before returning in search of greener pastures.

The pictures I conjured up in my mind were certainly not of the woman sitting across from me. My origin was seldom ever a subject of discussion at the house. I knew someone was responsible for my birth, and I was connected to Mpa and Nne through the said person. But that was about it.

The meeting was an awkward one, even for an eight-year-old. I greeted my mother again, this time, with a stutter.

"Ngozi nwa'm,"[20] she pulled me into an embrace.

I hugged her timidly. No one had addressed me by my legal first name outside formal settings in forever. My grandparents dubbed me Peppe, after the spicy berry, because I was as feisty as I was

---

[20] "Ngozi, my child."

hardworking. Everyone at the village knew me by the nickname too, save for school, where the authorities addressed me formerly.

"Look at your siblings, Chidinma and Bobo," said my mom, breaking the hug.

I nodded feebly, bereft of how best to address them. The only sibling I'd grown up to know was an older sister who had relocated back to the city before we were even old enough to understand each other or form a relationship. I could barely recall the details of her looks and sometimes, she seemed like the fictitious conjuration of a childish mind wanton from loneliness. If anyone else recalled this sister of mine, they barely showed. Not my grandparents or peers or the rest of the villagers appeared to remember the time that was. It was just me now—Ngozi Peppe, granddaughter of Mpa Akuozor and Nne Udeozor.

The grown-ups soon began to talk again, allowing me enough time to slip away. I returned to the usekwu, hands trembling, heart thumping loudly in my chest, and went through the dishes in a blitz.

After a hurried bath, I slipped into my best dress, which paled in comparison to what my newfound family were garbed in. My siblings looked bored sucking on tiny straws sticking out of juice boxes and glancing around the house. It seemed unbelievable that two little kids were allowed to have whole beverages all to themselves, let alone two different packs. I couldn't recall the last time I had any decent beverage that wasn't the locally made drink wrapped in cellophane and frozen solid. *Condense*, we called it.

Quickly overcoming my timidity and feeling a little confident in myself now that I'd changed into slightly better clothes, my mom allowed me to steal Chidinma and Bobo momentarily, with the promise that I wouldn't stray too far from the house or put them in harm's way. I readily agreed, eager to show off my beautiful siblings to my friends. No more would I be regarded as the girl with no brother(s) or sister(s). Now, I had two to call mine, and beautiful ones too.

Everywhere I called, my friends were too stunned to believe or too embarrassed to indulge me for long. But I was excited beyond understanding or care. For once, the tables had turned, and I got to watch the jealousy on their faces.

That's right. This girl also has siblings.

The adults were biding their time when I got back with the kids. Some dirty dishes sat on a tray atop a tiny kitchen stool, indicating that the women had shared a meal. Nne was reclining in Mpa's lounge chair, and my mom looked relaxed, slouching in the worn-out armchair.

"Peppe, ọ bụ gị?[21]" Nne said as I pandered into the room.

"Eh,"[22] I replied, letting go of my siblings who ran to our mother.

I started to tidy the plates when my grandmother stopped me.

"Peppe mba nu,"[23] Nne sprang upright, catching my hands. "No worry about the plates. Nne gị na akpọrọ gị gaa n'obodo[24]."

My heart picked a new rhythm. I turned to look at my mom who was too engrossed with my siblings to see me biting back a smile. Nne gave me the nod to go tidy up myself. She needn't tell me twice. I dashed out of the living area to the tiny room we shared, rummaging through piles of overgrown and spoilt shoes that littered the underside of Nne's sagging bed. I found a pair that I seldom ever wore save for very special occasions, like Christmas and Easter.

The shoes had aged poorly with torn inner linings and an ill-fitting sole from too many visits to the local cobbler. The body was no better—a faded;

---

[21] "Peppe, is that you?"
[22] Pidgin "Yes."
[23] "Peppe, don't—"
[24] "Your mother is taking you to town."

ashy shadow was all that remained of the bright, shiny black that it used to be. It cramped my toes when I wore it, having outgrown it by two years. But it was the best in my collection of harrowing footwear. With some effort, I tugged on the shoes, wincing back to the living room.

The shock and sadness that crossed my mom's face the instant she saw me couldn't be missed. For the first time, her large, black eyes held anything but laughter. What's regret to an eight-year-old who knew no more than happiness or sadness, white or black?

Of Blinding Lights and Fine Places

I'd never seen a woman drive anything beyond a motorbike until my mom. I didn't know she came in a car until we made it out of the village.

"The roads are deplorable, so I couldn't take the risk," she explained as though reading my thoughts.

Deplorable, I tossed the word around in my mind. *What could that mean?*

My mom was first to alight from the motorcycle that brought us to her hotel on the outskirts of the village. It was a world of its own out there, unlike anything in my small, comely village—

complete with overhead lights and heavy traffic. I'd never seen so many automobiles in one place before. Honks rent the air, the sound of tires grounding across asphalt too. The only vehicles that dared to ply the wretched roads of Okohia were huge construction machines that came to dredge the nearby river and tankers ferrying water between little, landlocked communities. Other than that, very few folks owned vehicles, as the common mode of transportation was walking, cycling, or motorbiking.

Above the din of vehicles was music booming from several large speakers lining the bush bar of the hotel. I'd never been outside of the village before, and certainly not near this much civilization. Everything had a new, different feel and look to it. The houses were bigger, fancier, and more expressive as though moulded with the best materials and structural finesse.

Awed to no small degree, I perused the landscape with a keen eye, beaming to myself at the stories I'd tell my peers.

This Peppe is no regular girl again. I've seen the light.

Mom discontinued my drunken worship of the surroundings, shooing us into the establishment and pandering behind like an overprotective hen. We made for a stairwell and pranced up to a room. She withdrew a key from the corner of her purse and jammed it into the lock. After a couple of clicks, the door fell open. Mom flicked a switch and the lights came on, bathing the room in a soft, white glow. A ceiling fan blew quietly. A medium-sized bed, perhaps the main furniture in the room, sat next to a window overlooking the busy street. Two bedside tables sat on either side, one holding a small clock and the other an organizer for pens or toothbrushes.

A giant suitcase sat on the bed, partly closed. Mom placed her purse on one of the bedside tables as my siblings clambered onto the bed.

"Get down, you guys, we won't be long."

Chidinma and Bobo obeyed without a fuss, climbing down the side of the bed until their tiny feet touched the thick woollen carpeting. The flooring of the hotel was another source of marvel for me.

Who knew you could hide the entire floor of a room!

I was still mushing my feet into the fabric of the carpet when mom tapped me on the shoulder.

"Let's go, Ngo."

***

Mom handled the wheel with clinical precision, rounding bends and switching lanes like a driving whiz. It was like the movies I saw with my friends from the broken rear window of Papa

Ifeanyi's house. My siblings occupied the owner's area, while I strapped in next to my mom in the passenger's seat. The journey was mostly quiet, save the voice of my mom quietly humming to a song on the stereo. Chidinma and Bobo soon dozed off, while I peered around and outside the car, my eyes gleaming in excitement.

The drive was starting to near the half an hour mark when mom pulled into an outlandish eatery. *Mr Biggs*, it read, in some of the boldest, brightest letters I'd ever seen. Mom helped to undo my seatbelt before alighting to wake my siblings, who mumbled and sleepwalked their way into the building. It was considerably cooler inside like it was about to rain. Only the sky was outside, clear and sunny as can be. But no one seemed to be bothered by the cold.

I ran my hands across my arms, shrugging slightly. My thin clothes were as much help as a hand fan to putting out a wildfire. My family, though, didn't seem to notice the sudden drop in temperature. If anything, my siblings were wide awake now, eagerly pointing to the kiddies' area and haggling our mom into letting them go. She ignored them, strutting across the beautifully tiled floors to the food counter.

"What'd you like, Bobo?"

"Mince pie and ice cream," the toddler declared emphatically, flashing tiny rows of dentition.

"Mommy, me too," Chidinma chimed, pressing her face against the transparent showcase of the food counter.

Mom got around to placing orders without bothering to ask for my opinion. Not that I know what I'd have picked anyway. The array of foods all looked strange and tantalizing, I could never agree on one. Even my siblings' choice sounded bizarre to me, never mind knowing what I wanted.

"We'll be at…" Mom said to one of the servers, craning her neck to catch the number of a table some yards away. "Table 5. That one there." She pointed.

No sooner had we assumed the table than our meals were brought in. Chidinma and Bobo were served identical dishes, while a large plate of fried rice and chicken was placed in front of me at the directives of my mother.

"They did not bring anything for you," I declared in a quiet voice, staring down at my food.

I sounded local in comparison to my siblings, who spoke in much softer voices devoid of dialectical interference.

"Ngo, don't worry about me. I'm still full from earlier."

"Is only me one that have this food?" My gaze flitted between the plate and my mom.

"Yes, Ngo," she bit back a smile.

My brows furrowed in confusion. I had a whole plate of rice and chicken to myself. Never in the history of meat-eating had I been privileged to eat an entire piece of chicken. Usually, on the rare occasions when Nne deigned to prepare a meal with one of her chickens, I only got a tiny piece, which she bit out of hers while eating. If I was super lucky, Mpa would hand me his leftovers. But, even then, it was more bones and marrow than meat. Not that I knew enough to complain or want more though.

"Thank you, ma," I smiled broadly.

Mom smiled back, encouraging me to eat as she opened a pack of juice and filled a glass. The day ended on a high with small talk flying across the table.

Evening clouds were starting to ferry across the sky when we made our way back to the hotel. The next two days I spent with my family flew by in a blur. I was more confident around them and had bonded well with my siblings. I filled their imaginations with tales of the village and they told me about city life.

For once, everything seemed to be working out. I was the happiest I'd ever been, with my family's company. But this happy chapter of my life was but a short phase, which would give way to a much darker future.

During the third day of my stay, Nne showed up at the hotel. I knew something was up when I watched mom pack her bags and ready the kids. I'd been given a bag myself, with several new stuff and goodies to share with my peers.

"Nne, have you come to stay with us?"

My grandmother chuckled heartily.

"Na so the thing sweet you reach, eh, Peppe?"

I couldn't place what she was on about, so I turned to my mom.

"We're heading back to Lagos, Ngo," she said, dragging my otherwise dreamy vacation to a screeching halt.

"Am I following you people?"

The Man Called Father

Mpa Akuozor was a man of many troubles in his days. A good man well-beloved by his folks, sure, but tortured by life at every twist and turn. Until meeting my grandmother, Mpa suffered an unfair fate. Nne Udeozor was his third wife, not by choice but the unfortunate happenstance that his other wives died prematurely. But what my grandfather lacked in martial longevity, he made up for in children. His previous unions were all blessed with offsprings that lived longer than their mothers.

Given the circumstances of my birth, Mpa and Nne were the only immediate and present elderly figures in my life I could call parents.

It'd been years since my grandparents' marriage and even longer since the tragedy of Mpa's two wives; so, it was safe to assume that he had healed and moved on.

But had he truly?

At the time, it'd been about three years since I met my mother and siblings and I'd aged considerably. They kept in touch for the first few months and I was ecstatic to hear from them regularly. But the calls dried up with each passing year and with it my enthusiasm. Now, all my mother's calls were with her parents. Any mention of me was as an oversight, or just as the conversation drew to an end.

Consequently, the buzz surrounding my mom's return had died around the village and life continued with an unforgiven consistency. Then all was still the night Nne took ill. It seemed like regular malaria at first, presenting symptoms of headaches, body aches, and fever. As always, we sought out the village chemist for over-the-counter drugs. But Nne didn't seem to be getting better with each passing day, unnerving my grandfather.

Around the fourth day into the illness, he hovered over his wife, pressing wet, balled-up pieces of rags against her face and neck. His eyes looked sunken and vacant, and there was an uneasiness about his gait. Mpa tossed the rags into a nearby bucket, easing himself onto a tiny stool hitched to Nne's bed. The couple whispered to themselves, while my grandmother replied in groans and wisps.

"Peppe?" it was Mpa.

I rose from my position next to the door, strutting to his side.

"Ana m eburu Nne n'ụlọ ọgwụ. Gaa n'ụlọ Papa Okafor gwaa ya ka o jiri ọgba tum tum ya bịa[25]."

With a nod and one final glance at my grandmother, I sped out of the house.

---

[25] "I'm taking Nne to the hospital. Go to Papa Okafor's house and tell him to come with his motorcycle."

28

***

Nne was hospitalized for some medical complications my grandfather could neither comprehend nor pronounce. For he returned with a long face and offered little to no explanation as to what was wrong with Nne or how long she would be away.

Now, Mpa was an aged man who couldn't make the long trip to the hospital every day; so, he relied on news from his older children and their families. Unfortunately, as is with third-party communication, everyone returned with different kinds of news, which didn't serve to allay his fears.

I watched my grandfather grow distant and sorrowful—a far cry from the once warm and vibrant person he used to be. Soon, he stopped going out, choosing instead to hide away in his room. Many a time, I caught him between a soliloquy or sulking, calling on his ancestors and questioning his chi[26].

He stopped receiving guests too, bidding me tell them off with a lie of his unavailability. Weeks rolled into a month since Nne was admitted at the hospital and Mpa had grown skeletal from overthinking and starvation. He'd gone from eating little to flat out rejecting meals. His children who

---

[26] God

called at the house to check up on him and brief him on Nne's progress soon found out and chided him. To ensure he ate, my uncles' wives took turns coming around to prepare his meals.

A man in pain, sure, but Mpa was also as virtuous as they came. He couldn't rubbish the efforts of his daughters-in-law; so, he stopped rejecting his meals, although he never really ate them either. When the final bits of food had been served and the cookware washed and turned over, and my aunts returned to their homes, Mpa would call me to his room. There, he handed me the food, untouched, offering a weak smile to deter me from any questions.

Being somewhat naïve to care, I accepted the food and treated myself to a feast. It was an enjoyable cycle. Then, one night, my aunts served Mpa his meal and left. I waited for his signal, which didn't fail to come.

"Peppe!" his voice croaked into the night.

"Mpa'm!"[27] I raced blindly towards his room, grabbing some leftover wraps of fufu from the usekwu.

I entered the musty room illuminated by a tiny kerosene lamp. He pointed at a platter balanced

---

[27] "My father!"

on an upturned mortar, which held an inviting sight of well-garnished *oha soup*[28]. I hurried out of the room; a broad grin plastered to my face. As I devoured the dish with reckless abandon, my aunts returned shortly afterwards, having forgotten to brief Mpa on Nne's condition. No sooner had they called at papa's room than I heard a shrill cry.

I paused to listen, a morsel of fufu clinging to the roof of my mouth.

"Peppe!!!" It was one of my aunts.

I jumped slightly, almost choking on the food I was yet to swallow.

"Ma!" I managed after chugging down some water.

One of the women caught me as I entered the lobby.

"Kedu ebe I no, nwa a? Mee ngwa ngwa n'ụlọ nwanne nna gị."[29]

---

[28] Local delicacy made with the African Rosewood plant.
[29] "Where is this child? Hurry up and go fetch your uncle."

The End of an Era

Several relatives had convened at the house and no one was allowing me to see Mpa. There were at least twenty heads, by my count. Instead, I'd been sent on several errands to the provision store and the chemist to procure drugs and some beverages. From the whispered conversations of my aunts and uncles, I picked up something along the lines of Mpa not feeling well. I couldn't have been more perplexed.

The same Mpa that gave me his food only minutes ago? Mba nu nau[30].

I returned to Nne's room to clear out the dishes, having lost the will and desire to continue eating. The relatives that'd previously filled Mpa's room were starting to fan out, spilling into the spacious backyard and living area. There was a slight sense of relief between them, and they soon took to talking among themselves, their voices echoing into the moonlit night. I seized the moment to sneak past them into my grandfather's room, where I found the aged man fast asleep in his lounge chair with a wet cloth covering his collarbone and upper torso.

"Mpa?" I whispered, watching for onlooking or eavesdropping relatives.

---

[30] Inflected form of now

Silence.

"Mpa?" I ventured closer to him and touched his arm.

Nothing.

"Mpa bu lie?"[31] my voice was slightly higher this time, concern getting the better of me.

Usually, my grandfather snored in his sleep and stirred whenever I mentioned his name. But he was rather quiet and didn't budge under my touch.

A relative must have heard me, because several of them entered the room immediately, bringing in a large hurricane lamp they'd lit.

"Peppe, gịnị ka ọ bụ?"[32] it was one of my uncles.

"Mpa anaghị aza."[33]

The women among them shooed me out of the room, shutting the door. The remaining relatives in the yard soon started to troop in, questioning me as they headed for Mpa's room.

"Ọ dị mma eh, Peppe?"[34]

_____

[31] "Get up, Mpa."
[32] "Peppe, what is it?"
[33] "Mpa isn't responding"

33

I stared at them blankly, mute and incapable of stringing my thoughts coherently. All I knew was that my grandfather didn't respond to my calls. I was scared to imagine the unthinkable, which played around the circumference of my mind.

The door slammed again, shutting me out of the unfolding drama in Mpa's room. I heard a whimper, a welp, then a sniffle.

"Nwanyi, kpara onwe gi agwa!"[35] A male voice crooned. It sounded angry like one of the women was acting out of line.

What could have possibly warranted such a chiding, my young mind pondered.

The occupants soon began conversing amongst themselves, but I could barely understand them even with my ear pressed to the door. In the brevity of the moment, the door flung open and I staggered into the room. A pair of powerful arms flashed before my eyes, saving me from an imminent collision with the ground.

It was Mpa's oldest son, Bonny.

"Peppe, ebee ka nna m na-edebe mmanya ya?"[36]

---

[34] "Is all well, Peppe?"
[35] "Woman, pull it together!"
[36] "Peppe, where does my father keep his drinks?"

No one seemed to mind that I'd been attempting to eavesdrop on a private conversation. It was hard to make out everyone's expression in the overcrowded room, but I could tell all was not well. For starters, why would my uncle be interested in his father's drinks? And why did my aunts look away when I stepped in, wiping their faces with the ends of their wrappers?

Pushing away from his arms, I smoothed down my dress. At this point, it was impossible to focus, what with the stifled commotion playing out before me.

"Peppe!"

I jumped slightly, stuttering and pointing blindly at several parts of the room.

"In the up side," I finally gestured at the ramshackle wardrobe sitting against the wall of Mpa's room.

The room started to clear out, with several relatives stepping out in groups of twos or threes until there were just Mpa's oldest sons—Bonny and Kevin—and I left. No one attempted to send me out of the room. I watched Uncle Bonny push the upturned mortar against the wardrobe and reached for a bottle of local gin.

They both knelt next to my grandfather who I noticed for the first time had been laid out on his bed.

He was reclining in his lounge chair the last time I saw him.

"Ezumike, Papa. Nwee udo,"[37] Bonny drizzled the liquor around Mpa's bed in obeisance.

"Uncle, what happened to Mpa?" tears started to fill my eyes.

He ignored me, continuing to go round his father's bed several times, pouring libation. He stopped at the foot of the bed and bowed one last time.

"Agu!"[38] Kevin saluted. "Ijeoma!"[39]

Tears were streaming down my face as I connected the dots. No one could muster the courage to tell me, so they let me find out for myself.

"What now?" I croaked, watching my uncle douse Mpa's body with the rest of the gin.

Uncle Bonny turned to look at me for the first time since I tripped, a sad sigh escaping his lips. I saw the helplessness on his face. No one was prepared for Mpa's demise. Not me nor his oldest child. Sometimes, even adults wished they had all the answers.

---

[37] "Rest well, father. Go in peace."
[38] "The tiger!" (Reverence of strength)."
[39] "Safe journey!"

For Lack of a Better Time

Mpa was buried the following day in a quiet event attended by several close relatives and friends. The news of his demise was whispered across the village, which incurred me their pity. Nne's health was now a second priority as relatives did the most to fulfil the final rites of their kinsman.

Bags hung beneath my eyes and my appetite waned as the days passed. Living alone in the house without Nne and Mpa was torture. Several aunts and uncles tried to get me to stay with them, but I always returned to my grandparents', Mpa's room precisely, where I cried myself to sleep. They gave up at some point, allowing me to grieve at my pace.

One fine morning, I woke up to the sound of the neighbours exchanging pleasantries with a familiar voice.

"Nne, ututu oma!"[40]

My eyes fluttered open and I cocked my head to listen. The voice drew closer to the house.

"Peppe nwa'm!"[41]

---

[40] "Nne, good morning!"
[41] "Peppe, my child."

I stumbled to my feet, dashing through the door towards the front of the house. There, I found my Nne, all smiles and strutting towards the house with some relatives in tow. I leapt into her arms, sending her staggering backwards.

"Nne'm!"[42]

"Peppe nwa'm," she smiled down at me.

I saw the tears in her eyes and the happiness on her face. Nne was glad to be back. Glad that she returned healthier than she left. Glad that there was no love lost in her absence.

But I doubted she'd heard the news. Why else would she be so happy? And why were the relatives with her except to convey the sad news?

"Nne, Mpa anwuọla,"[43] fresh tears choked my words. I buried my head into her stomach.

"Tah! Mechie onu gi, nwa a!"[44] it was Uncle Kevin. "Nne, no mind am."

Nne turned sharply, giving him a thorough stare down.

---

[42] "My mother."
[43] "Papa is dead."
[44] "Keep quiet, child."

"Ọ bụrụ na ọ bụ onye ụgha, gịnị kpatara o ji adị gị ngwa ngwa imechi ya,"[45] she sounded fierce. Returning her attention to me, her voice softened. "Peppe, kedu ihe I kwuru?"[46]

"Mpa anwụọla," my lips trembled, breaking my words into a stutter.

Nne fell backwards but was caught by the relatives.

"Chineke, gịnị ka m mehiere?"[47] she wailed, sinking into the dust. I dropped down next to her, making a pillow on her legs, our voices chorusing in an uneven medley of lamentations.

***

Life with Nne didn't last long before another event threatened to pull us apart. We'd been managing through each day, feeling the brunt of Mpa's absence with every blow life dealt us. Now, I no longer had a father. Not one to tell me stories beneath starry, moonlit nights; make me brooms from raffia; or defend me from my grandmother's cane.

---

[45] "If she is such a liar, why are you quick to silence her?"
[46] "What did you say?"
[47] "God, what is my wrongdoing?"

No thanks to her illness, Nne wasn't as fit as she used to be. She couldn't stand for long or attempt several activities she once undertook with finesse. Now, all of those chores fell to me. I didn't mind the new workload, but there was only so much my young shoulders could bear at any one point. My mom saw this too, for she sent for Nne a little after the latter had mourned her husband.

The news hit home with a wave of relief. Nne seemed genuinely happy at the chance to catch a break. But the prospect of seeing the grand city of Lagos was the more interesting perk for me. Mom had given us two days to prepare, and it was all I could do to daydream of the things I'd do and see in the city. Leaving the confines of my tiny village that one time had fuelled my imaginations, I couldn't help it.

Some 48 hours and a huge dose of restlessness later, and the D-day was upon us. Some relatives came over to help with the packing, one of which was Uncle Bonny. He seemed to be more present in our lives now that my grandfather was gone. I busied myself getting dressed and putting the usekwu in order before the trip. The sound of engine revving in the compound announced the arrival of the motorcycle that would take us to the bus park.

My uncle chose that moment to send me on an errand, directing me to go fetch his phone. Now,

Uncle Bonny lived some 20 to 30 minutes away from us; so, it was not going to be an easy journey on foot. I hurried out, nosing my way through the village, and made the journey back in a fraction of the time. But when I returned, neither Nne nor the motorcycle was in the compound. The house had also been locked up, and my uncle sat in front awaiting my return, a bottle of beer nesting next to him.

"Ebee ka Nne?"[48] I queried.

He ignored my question, rising to his feet, beer in hand.

"Ka anyị laa nụlọ."[49]

Of Tears and Happily Ever Afters

To say I felt betrayed by my grandmother would be an understatement. I was mad. But I wasn't cross with Nne alone. I also resented my mother. How could she claim to be a parent and leave me behind? Whatever happened to a mother's love? It sickened me to think of her. How I'd been played me into believing she was a good person, what with how she treated me when we first met. I chided myself for expecting too much of someone who I didn't know

---

[48] "Where is Nne?"
[49] "Let's go home."

until I was eight. What had I had to look forward to but disappointment?

Uncle Kevin said something about my mom giving birth as the reason for Nne's visit, but that didn't serve to assuage my fury one bit.

Did I not deserve to see my new sibling or know our father? Why would I be left behind like a second thought with no plans whatsoever?

In a desperate show of retribution, I took out my rage on relatives who tried to help. I changed houses at regular intervals, not for the fun of it, but because relatives took the liberty to maltreat and overwork me. It didn't make sense that they'd try to punish me for wrongdoings afterwards; so, I bailed often, going through relatives with such vengeance.

Within the first month that Nne was gone, I became truant and grew wild and out of control, living up to the nickname Mpa had given me. Relatives soon gave up trying to bridle me and shipped me off to go live with one of my mom's sisters.

Aunty Livina lived in Amaigbo, another area of Imo state, with her kids, husband, and an in-law. She was a no-nonsense woman with a penchant for rewarding every behaviour accordingly. As a result, I had to succumb.

Her intervention couldn't have been timelier. I was enrolled in a school and groomed to improve my English. Unlike my school in the village, the new school didn't resort to the local dialect; everything was conducted in English. Back at home, Aunt Livina fostered my fluency in the language by seldom ever conversing in Igbo, even though her household was well-versed in the local dialect.

Unlike her other siblings, Aunt Livina was learned and worked as a nurse; hence, her higher standards for me and her children. There was a sense of stability with my aunt that I didn't get elsewhere. There, I wanted to grow and put the past behind me. It felt great to not be worried for a minute.

Life continued on this stable plane for another 11 months until Nne returned from her trip to the city. I was hesitant to return to the village after the last stint, but my grandmother was old and incapable of living on her own.

***

The reunion was messier than I envisioned. I imagined I'd still be resentful towards Nne and give her the cold shoulder. But all that attitude melted away, and I crumbled at her feet and wept. I cried like I was five again: sober and remorseful and in need of petting. She cried too, patting my back and reassuring me of her return.

Nne had shrunk since the last time we met. There was a slight hunch to her frame, and her gait was a little slower and shakier now. The silver streaks that used to be in her hair now stretched the entire length of her crown.

I refrained from asking about my mom or siblings, having made up my mind that I was unwanted and therefore, unloved by them. Nne seemed to sense my sentiments and steered clear off the subject. We soon settled into the hustle and bustle of village life again, making the most of Mpa's absence. In the space of two years, we'd downsized from being a family of three to two; and I'd gone from bettering my English to returning to the dumps that ruined it.

It took another year before I heard from my mom again. This time, she wanted Nne to come to visit, but with me this time.

"Ngo, you will come to Lagos with Nne," mom said over the phone.

My resolve failed, breaking out in a sheepish smile as I pressed Uncle Kevin's phone to my ear. He'd brought the news and had rung mom when he arrived.

"True, true?" I asked, twirling my feet in the sand.

"Honest," her voice was crisp.

The smile grew into a soft chuckle and then full-blown laughter.

"Nne, I'm going to Lagos," I handed the phone to my uncle and rushed over to my grandmother, my eyes glistening with tears.

She rubbed my head without a word and stared fixedly at the setting sun banking in the horizon. We shared a companionable silence, ruptured only by the sound of Kevin's motorcycle revving out of the compound.

3

VILLAGE GIRL TO THE WORLD!

"Peppe, tukwuru ala!"[50] Nne chuckled, patting the seat beside her.

I tore my gaze from the window, flashing my grandmother a quick smile before ignoring her altogether and continuing with my sightseeing. The Coaster bus bounced softly as it navigated the worn,

---

[50] "Sit down!"

pothole-ridden road, slowing down and picking up speed once it reached a decent patch of asphalt. The vehicle was quiet, save the whirring of the engine, which faded into the background as one got accustomed to it. The passengers were caught up in several indulgences: some sleeping, others tapping away at their phones or viewing the passing landscape.

There were a handful of kids on board too, but none shared in my euphoria. Not that I cared. I was too caught up in the moment to bother about what other passengers made of me. I'd already attracted stares from the neighbours on the adjacent seat, who were less than amused by my staccato squeals and frantic pointing. It was my first time in such a vehicle enroute to the big city of Lagos; I had every right to express myself.

Nne and I were accompanied by my uncle Mom had sent to fetch us. He dozed off for the most part of the trip, and when he wasn't almost falling off his seat in slumber, he browsed his cell phone and made loud calls. Nne slept at some point, probably tired from trying to get me to sit down. She was an old woman and couldn't keep up with my boisterousness after all.

The journey lasted several hours, with two stops along the way for passengers to ease themselves and grab some refreshments. It was late afternoon when we arrived in Lagos. I don't know what I expected of the metropolitan state, but it definitely didn't involve hordes of people going in different directions all at once. It was choreographed chaos! There was neither lull nor a definite sound, but a cacophony of blaring honks, animal cries, metal- and woodworks, and generator noises.

The driver nosed the vehicle into a bus park and the door hissed open. Passengers poured out, going around the vehicle to collect their luggage. Nne held my wrist with a death grip, as we trailed behind Uncle Chibuike, who joined the crowd of chattering passengers to get our things. Soon, we were stuffed into a taxi and underway to my mother's residence.

The cab pulled up next to a huge gate and my uncle got out, coming round to help Nne and me out of the vehicle. He collected our baggage from the booth and settled the fare before pushing a button from a switch hanging from the wall. I stared in wonder as he pushed the button again, looking to Nne for clues. My grandmother didn't seem to be bothered about whatever Uncle Chibuike was up to, instead, staring at me with a cheeky grin.

"Peppe nke na-anọghị na bọs,"[51] she swung my arm softly.

---

[51] "Peppe that refused to sit on the bus."

I turned away to hide my smile, trying to withdraw my hand, but Nne held on and continued teasing. The squealing of metal disrupted our little moment, as the gate peeled open to reveal Chidinma and Bobo. They bounded towards Nne and hugged her tightly.

"Umụ m[52], how una dey?" she rubbed their heads, looking down at their upturned faces.

"Fine," they chorused, turning to me.

I held out my arms and they walked into my embrace. I pressed them to myself, burying my face between their heads. Both my siblings had hit their growth spurts and were almost twice their heights the last we saw. Chidinma was almost as tall as I was.

Uncle Chibuike ushered us into the house amidst the pleasantries and chit chat between Nne and my siblings. Left to my thoughts, I drank in the sights of my mom's house. The compound was spacious, with the building set up towards the far end. A tree sat to the eastern end of the gate, providing shade to mom's car parked underneath its luscious canopy. The rest of the compound was covered in interlocking tiles, with bits of grass stubbornly growing through the cracks of the layout.

----

[52] "My children."

The interior of the house was even more impressive, boasting polished tile floors and neatly painted walls. No sooner had the door shut behind us than I heard mom's voice as she descended from the stairwell.

"Nne'm, nnọọ,"[53] she curtseyed.

Nne pulled her daughter up for a hug, patting mom on the back softly.

"Daalụ o. Kedu ka ị mere?"[54]

Mom nodded, grinning broadly. She looked in my direction, beckoning on me. I strutted to her side and flung myself at her.

"Chi m! Ngo, i toro ibu o,"[55] she exchanged glances with Nne, who smiled at us.

"Sister, good afternoon," Uncle Chibuike entered the living room, heading towards the room reserved for Nne with our baggage.

"Ehen, my brother. Kedu?"[56]

"I dey."

---

[53] "Welcome, mother."
[54] "Thanks. How are you?"
[55] "My god! Ngo, you have grown big."
[56] "How are you?"

"Ngo, you're home now, inu? Welcome to Lagos!" Mom patted my head before turning to my sister. "Take her to the room and tell Grace that Nne has arrived; so, she should hurry up."

Chidinma latched onto my arm and pulled me the entire way to the kitchen, which sat behind the living area. Inside, some petite lady laboured over a countertop slicing some leaves and humming quietly.

"Auntie Grace, see my sister!" Chidinma declared proudly, nudging me forward.

"Good afternoon, ma," I stammered, unsure of how to proceed.

"Afternoon," she rinsed her hands, wiping it on her apron. "Chi, you didn't even tell me that you had a big sister," the house help chided Chidinma before flashing me a smile. "How are you, my dear?"

I nodded, returning a smile of my own. Her eyes seemed to be gobbling me up, surprise evident in her lingering stare. Chidinma delivered mom's message and saw me off to the room they had prepared for me.

"Where will you and Bobo na sleep?" I sank into the plush mattress, sizing up the room.

Chidinma sniggered. "We have our room."

The thought of my little siblings having a large room all for themselves struck me as odd as I shut the door behind Chidinma who left to answer mom's call, returning to the bed where I ran my fingers across its silky sheets and polished wooden frame. The room was elaborately furnished, but not so much so that it bordered on the extreme. Nonetheless, that was the most luxury I'd seen in any one place designated to me. Thoughts about Nne's room briefly filtered through my mind, but I quickly disposed of them.

If I could have a room of my own, Nne was well catered for.

I should get out of my clothes, I decided, collecting my thoughts.

Suddenly, it struck me that Nne hadn't packed my stuff; hence, our little baggage. I figured she was following my mother's instructions. Last I saw the woman, she gave me quite the treat.

Now to freshen up and take a tour of the house.

***

"We don't have a stream here," Auntie Grace chuckled, almost toppling over in laughter.

I couldn't understand her amusement.

"But I want to baff," I blurted out unamused.

She took a moment to pull herself together, taking quick deep breaths to calm herself.

"We don't use a stream, my dear. There's water in the house," she explained with a bit of effort, biting back laughter. "There's water in the tap."

I was fascinated by the magic of plumbing.

"So, you people don't use to go outside and fetch water?

She shook her head, returning to the sink where she flipped a lever and out gushed water to my amazement.

"Ewoo!"[57] my eyes were the size of saucers. "Auntie, gimme bucket let me take water," I glanced around.

I was really pushing Auntie Grace to the edge with my ignorance. She was trying so hard not to laugh.

"Come with me," she led out of the kitchen and through the lobby and headed for my room. She turned the knob and left the door ajar. I trailed

---

[57] "Wow!"

behind her until she stopped behind a door on the left end of the room.

"This is the bathroom," she pushed the door open.

True to her words, the neatest washroom I'd ever seen came into view complete with immaculate white, tiled walls and a water closet. It was the second time I'd get to use a proper toilet after the one at my mom's hotel room years ago. Back in the village, taking a dump was done by squatting over a pit latrine made of mud. It was no comfortable place, what with the flies it attracted in their droves; so, time was of the essence.

But this bathroom... I could sleep in it just fine. It looked like something out of a magazine.

"I'm not seeing any tap here," I observed, craning my neck.

"You can go in," Auntie Grace beckoned. "There's a tap under the shower," my gaze followed her pointing hand.

"But you won't have to use it."

"Ahahn. How will I now baff?"

By now, all her laughter was gone and she regarded me with a bit of pity in her eyes. She took off her flip-flops and stepped into the bathroom, skulking towards the shower. Auntie Grace pointed at a lever before giving it a full 360-degree turn. The sound of water gurgling in the piping struck my ears, just before it started to rain from the showerhead. The house help reversed the tap head, shutting off the water supply.

"What do you think?"

***

"Ngozi, jiri ya nwayọọ,"[58] Mom chided, watching me shove spoonfuls of rice into my mouth.

I was eating at a rather alarming pace, holding onto the bottle of Fanta I'd been served like it'd cease to exist if I let go. I slowed down to swallow, taking a long swig of the beverage.

"Enwere ihe ndị ọzọ n'ime ite ahụ,"[59] she balanced the glass on her nose.

Nne choked on her food from laughter. Mom patted her back and poured her some water. My grandmother looked up from her meal of eba[60] and

---

[58] "Take it easy."
[59] "There's still food left." (Second helpings)
[60] Doughy staple made from cassava flakes.

soup, regarding me with reddened eyes, a smile lingering on her lips.

"Ifeoma, biko hapu nwagboghobia ahu. Ọ ka na-enwe obi ụtọ,"[61] her voice was a little cracked from wheezing.

I continued my assault on the food, encouraged by Nne's comment in my defence. Mom didn't look too pleased with my table manners, but I was starving and bereft of any sense of self.

So far, I was enjoying my time in Lagos. I got a plate of food to myself, well-stocked with meats and other garnishing I could only dream of while at the village. Such foods only appeared on the pages of our textbooks and were heard of in the tall tales parried by children who couldn't admit that they'd had eba and leftover soup on Christmas morning.

With the availability of water in the house, bathing had become a luxury. The shower felt so good, it was like playing in the rain. I'd unintentionally stayed longer than necessary, missing Chidinma who came calling on me. My absence had sparked a bit of a stir, with everyone searching for me around the house until Auntie Grace told them where she last left me.

---

[61] "Ifeoma, please let her be. She's quite excited."

Chidinma had come knocking on the bathroom door to verify the information. It was some time before I heard the pounding above the splashing of water and answered from behind the door. I grabbed one of the thick, thirsty towels hanging from a rack and wrapped it around my tiny frame at the risk of looking like a burrito. Chidinma was gone by the time I emerged. I threw on the same clothes I'd worn earlier and exited the room. Mom and Nne were already at the table when I joined them in the dining area, with a covered plate sitting unattended. Mom gestured towards the dish and I took my place behind it.

By the time I was done with the meal, stomach rotund and protruding from overeating, I was quite groggy from jetlag and boisterousness. Auntie Grace came to clear the table just as I'd started to nod off, with Bobo entering the fray. He held a delicately bound wrap in his hand, which he promptly handed over to our mother before disappearing into the living room to watch TV.

"Ngo, come and see Mimi." It was mom.

My eyes shot open in an instant, my senses awakening to the babbling of a baby kicking and grabbing at the air. My baby sister was a bundle of cute and cuddly complete with pinchable cheeks, large brown eyes, and two pairs of tiny teeth.

Mom dropped her in my arms gently and Mimi cooed, sucking on her fingers and eyeing me with renewed interest. I smiled down at her and she returned one of her own, breaking out in staccato laughter. I raised her slightly until her upper torso was on my left shoulder, patting her diapered bottom. She squirmed in my arms with a little too much force that I expected of an infant. Mom reached out instinctively, withdrawing when she saw that I had the situation under control.

But Mimi had other ideas of her own. She let out a little whimper, forcing me to return to cradling her in my arms. Her face was contorted and tears glistened in her eyes.

"Ndo,"[62] I shushed, swinging her softly from side to side.

The distraction seemed to be working and Mimi grew quieter. But no one could've predicted what happened next. In the brevity of the moment I glanced at Mom, who had barely taken her eyes off me, Mimi lurched her dinner at my face.

For the first time, I saw my mother throw back her head and laugh. I looked down at the tiny culprit, semi-digested formula and cereals dripping down my neck. She smiled. I smiled. All was forgiven.

---

[62] "Sorry."

Red Letter Day

The days rolled by and I adjusted to life in the city, although not all the way. I still woke up earlier than everyone else, Auntie Grace inclusive, and helped out with the chores. Even the promise of a luxurious life failed to rob me of my sense of duty.

According to mom's plans, Nne and I would remain in Lagos indefinitely as she was preparing to leave the country in pursuit of better opportunities. It seemed surreal to me that there was a much bigger place than Lagos out there.

The U.K., she'd called it, saying it meant some words that were out of my vocabulary and comprehension. She seemed so keen on the subject like there was something inherently wrong with Lagos that I neither noticed nor understood. I saw the fiery look in her eyes, which was something that rarely went away. Mom was one determined woman.

She'd taken me shopping the day after my arrival, stocking my wardrobe with all the clothes that were the rave at the time. She handed me several pairs of jeans to try on. But I was a little hesitant given that I belonged to a rosary unit back at the village church.

Hadn't the catechist said to only dress like the Holy Mary and shy away from worldly clothes, particularly trousers?

Mom was bemused by my hesitancy, more so by the reasons, but encouraged me to try them.

"There's nothing wrong with trousers."

She was assuring and I gave in. Besides, my younger sister always wore trousers. What could it hurt?

After the huge wardrobe change came the first major milestone in my life: puberty.

It was one of those Saturday mornings when the neighbourhood was quiet and everyone was indoors. Power was on and the air was filled with a symphony of whirring fans, humming refrigerators, and TVs playing quietly. I was sleeping in, exhausted from staying up late into the night watching cartoons, when the door opened with a creak. I awoke with a start, squinting at the blinding light of the bulb I'd failed to switch off.

Mom stood at the doorway, her eyes narrowing down on me.

"What's that on the bed?"

I followed her gaze to the huge patch of red stretched across the dazzling white bedspread. My head failed to conjure up any rational explanation for the rather alarming sight, so I panicked, throwing a blanket over it.

I had no idea what had happened and didn't want to risk being a liar if I'd had a momentary spell of madness I couldn't recall.

"Erm... I..." I stumbled out of bed, rubbing my eyes and yawning wildly.

Mom started in my direction, causing my heart rate to spike. I flinched as she reached out to touch me. She withdrew, gazing at me calmly.

"I'm not trying to beat you, Ngo."

"Okay, ma," my voice was nothing but a shaky whisper.

"Did you injure yourself last night? Or, did you spill something on the sheets?"

I stared back blankly, twirling the corners of my dress and shifting my weight uneasily. She seemed to grasp my silence and descended to my level of understanding.

"I merụrụ onwe gị ahụ?"[63]

I shook my head.

"I wusara ihe n'elu akwa?"[64]

I shook my head again.

She took several steps towards me and raised my gaze to meet hers. Her voice was low, her breath caressing my forehead and temples.

"I ka mamịrị n'elu akwa?"[65]

I eyed the floor, drawing patterns with my toes.

Mom spun me around and gasped. I shot her a questioning look before directing my gaze to the back of the dress. I found an even bigger, darker patch of red.

Now, I was truly confused. Fear started to creep in and I might have teared up a little from ignorance. Mom placed a hand on my head and pulled me to her blossom, hugging me tightly. I heard her sigh deeply. Calmly. Relieved.

Periods, she'd called the phenomenon. They were a part of me now.

---

[63] "Did you hurt yourself?"
[64] "Did you spill anything on the bed?"
[65] "Do you bed wet?"

A Price to Pay

As mom geared up to travel, I was enrolled in school. My English was terrible and my diction barely had any words in it, even though I was in my final year of primary school. I relied more on facial expressions and gestures than actual comprehension for the bulk of my interactions with my siblings and mother. Nne was the only one I understood and could understand me.

Mom took me to one of these large neighbourhood schools: Children Companion, located in Ogba, Ikeja. Immediately we arrived at the premises, we were directed to the Proprietor's office, where I was tested in Mathematics and English.

I couldn't have been more clueless!

The questions were otherworldly, for I could barely understand them enough to attempt the test.

"Chineke! Kedu ihe bụ ihe a?"[66] I mumbled repeatedly.

Unsurprisingly, the results came back poor.

---

[66] God! What is this?

The proprietor called in Mom and me to discuss the assessment, advising that I was better off repeating Classes Four to Six again. It was difficult keeping up with him, but from the way he spoke, I knew it wasn't good news. Mom relayed the information to me on the way home, stating my poor fluency in spoken and written English as a core factor.

It broke me and for the remainder of the journey, I wept bitterly.

I was around 11 or 12 at the time, which was already a pretty big age for Primary Six. What's more, Bobo, who I was older than by about six years, was in Primary Four. The horror!

I'd seen my first period already and puberty had kicked into gear; I'd easily be the *mama of the class*.[67] This realization saddened me even more, and I questioned the validity of coming to the city.

Was Lagos worth it? I pondered, toying with the idea of returning to the village to complete elementary school. But before my immature plans could take root, Mom travelled out and I was resigned to the fate of being my younger brother's classmate.

---

[67] Oldest female

My first day at the new school was bland and uneventful. I stood in line with the rest of the kids that would be my mates for the school year— adolescents at best, with the oldest among them being three to four years younger than me.

I struggled with identity and took forever to make friends, not for lack of social skills but for the shame of being the oldest in a class of younger kids. With my mom gone, there was no one to confide in, who could understand my problem. Nne was around but would never have understood the psychosocial problem I faced in the classroom. She was not literate nor did she understand how schools work, to begin.

On the other hand, the other person who might have understood my struggles a little was Uncle Chibuike. But he was usually out working more times than he was at home. It's a miracle how he ever got the time to come fetch Nne and me.

He left early for work, sometimes, even before us kids left for school, and returned late at night when we'd eaten and gone to bed. On Sundays, his only non-working days, Uncle Chibuike spent the bulk of the time sleeping in, so much so that he missed attending church with us until we didn't bother inviting him along again.

I learned to internalize my struggles and only ever divulged my pains to a neighbour who was caring enough to lend a listening ear. When it was clear that my situation was only as good as I'd make of it, I came to terms with the reality of things. It wasn't the best of terms, but it was better than pretending to myself that the village educational system was worth anything beyond the sphere of Okohia.

On the path to self-recovery, I found solace in doing what I did best: running the house. With Mom out of the picture, Uncle Chibuike entering and exiting the fray like a fart in the wind, and Nne being both aged and incapable of having coherent conversations with my rather westernized siblings, someone needed to steer the ship.

Naturally, I fit the role perfectly. I had plenty of experience managing the house in the village with and without my grandparents present. I'd also successfully survived the most radical period of my life (when Nne left for the city upon Mpa's death). So, a lot was going for me.

In my desperate pursuit of purpose, I became more of a substitute mother than an actual sibling to my younger ones. I spanked them when they erred and tried to get them to respect me enough to heed my biddings. Suffice it to say, I was terrible at the job. My siblings had had our mother all their lives and there was no way I could pull an act capable of rivalling her.

I made a routine of ensuring that they bathed regularly and ate decently before and after school and during bedtime hours.

Mini was still a toddler with all the curiosity of a cat and the self-restraint of a pelican eel. Hence, a danger to herself if left unsupervised. My reign started on a bumpy ride, which soon gave way for a much smoother one over time. I had to stop trying to be my mother, whilst also leading with my crude imaginations of what it meant to run a household and command respect.

A Surprise to End All Surprises

Two years went by in a blur, and the pains of starting all over had paid off. My command of English was better—a phenomenon that had done wonders for my confidence and self-esteem. At the time, I'd also nailed managing my siblings and the rest of the household to the point Auntie Grace was relieved of her duties. Mom felt we no longer needed the house help and terminated her contract.

Another major surprise was the re-emergence of my older sister, Chioma. She was no figment of my imaginations after all, but had been living someplace she didn't amply describe to us. It was hard not being the oldest sibling, but Chioma didn't mind me handling the affairs. She proved to be the ideal sibling: not getting in the way and doing her best to help out when necessary.

With all of us siblings complete, it was a full house at the time of my graduation. The school had totally revamped my academics, presenting me as a different individual to the one who enrolled years back. I had good grades to show for it, with my name ranking third on the Common Entrance result list.

The fulfilment it brought was numbing, and I could just feel myself floating on the satisfaction of never having to be within the walls of a primary school ever again. The experience had been worthwhile in the end, even though the process had been agonizing.

I remember the gossip around the class and the snide remarks from my mates, who couldn't wait to get one over me almost always.

You'd think children were saints!

How they regarded me with mocking eyes whenever Uncle Chibuike came to drop us off or pick us from school. I wasn't familiar with the city and couldn't risk coming to school on my own just to look cool or mature to a bunch of kids. But that didn't stop me from considering my options. Until learning to make friends and ignore the unnecessary hate levied against me, it hurt to be treated like a freak intended to be poked and prodded and made fun of.

But all that was behind me now!

Mom couldn't fly back to the country for my graduation and Uncle Chibuike had to work, so it was a relatively low-key affair, leaving me to celebrate my personal wins. Almost immediately, I started scouting for Secondary Schools to apply to within and outside the state. I was still weighing my options when Mom phoned in to congratulate me.

"Ngo, can you see why I told you not to worry about repeating classes?"

I grinned. "Yes, mommy. I see it now."

"Congratulations are in order, my dear. You did well and I'm proud of you and how far you have come."

It was impossible to stay still hearing those praises from my mom. I felt loved. Validated. Seen.

"Thanks, mommy. Anyway, so there's this secondary school that I want to apply for. It's in Ogun State—"

"Ngozi?"

I paused, surprised that she'd addressed me by my full name.

"Yes, mommy…?"

"You don't have to worry your head about secondary school. I'd like for you guys to come and continue your education here."

The words rang in my ears like the lulling effect of a pleasant dream. My jaw hung loose and no sound proceeded from my mouth. I turned to look at my siblings whose eyes were trained on me.

"What did she say?" It was Chidinma getting off the couch to stand next to me.

"Ngozi, what's going on?" Chioma followed after Chidinma.

Still too numb to speak or move, my older sister wrung the phone from my grip.

"Hello, mommy?"

"Ngozi?"

"No, it's Chioma."

***

The promise of schooling in the United Kingdom came with its own sacrifices. Mom didn't want us to enrol in a secondary school only to pluck us out when she was ready for the relocation.

"That'd be wasting money," she said.

So, we had to make do with a private tutor, just like the one Mom had hired to coach me in Primary Four. For the next five to seven months before our mother's return, tutorials and travel preparations were the order of the day.

Uncle Chibuike returned home early from work one day under the instructions of our mother. He was to take us to get our international passports. After several days of back and forth, we obtained the documents. Now, the easy part was done. Next came the hard bit: visa application.

Chioma seemed to know a great deal about embassies and how they worked for some reason, and; hence, was chosen to be the spokesperson of the group.

"Chioma is the oldest and she knows how the interviews go. So, you all keep quiet and let her do the speaking, inu?" Uncle Chibuike drilled us. "You still remember some of the questions from previous interviews, don't you?" He faced Chioma squarely.

She nodded.

"Good," he returned his attention to the row of young faces huddled around him. "Now, if you guys are asked general questions like, 'Why do you all want to go to the U.K.?' What will your answer be?"

"Because my mommy said to come over?" It was Bobo.

"Nah!" Uncle Chibuike shook his head. "Too weak. Any trafficking victim could string the same line. Perhaps, why'd your mom want you guys coming on an international flight with no adult supervision? Chioma, any ideas?"

"Not really?"

"Okay. So, this should be your reply to that question: 'Because we miss our mommy.'"

He looked across our faces but saw no tinge of disagreement. With that, we were off to the embassy to apply for visas.

The embassy was filled with others like us, and it took a while before we were shown in. You'd be surprised how many people wanted to leave the country.

Uncle Chibuike didn't follow us in because we needed to be interviewed independently to ascertain we weren't being taken abroad illegally. The interviewer doled out questions, which Chioma answered with relative ease and confidence. I was proud of my sister, wherever she got her knowledge from.

True to my uncle's words, we were asked a variety of general questions. Mimi sat astride my laps, playing with her teddy bear and babbling to herself the entire time. As soon as we mentioned missing our mother as the main reason for our visa application, her interest was piqued.

"Mommy..." Mimi glanced at the interviewer, and then at me.

I smiled down at her, but she was rather forlorn and did not return the gesture.

"Ngo, I want to meet mommy."

The interviewer was amused and dismissed us without further questions. We returned to our uncle and started the long, feverish wait for the results.

It wasn't until a week later that Mom phoned in and told us that the visa application had been successful.

"Does it mean we can now come with you?" I gasped into the mouthpiece.

"Yes, my dear," she chuckled. "I'm done setting up here. I shall start processing my return soon."

Music to my ears.

Of Plated Worms and Emotional

Attachments

Mom's return was marked by excitement and a frenzy of preparation. Her flight landed the night before and she'd lodged at a hotel before making it home by dawn. Among the treats she got us was pasta—a strange dish I hadn't had the pleasure of eating ever; not as a village girl or as a refined, city one. If my siblings shared my excitement about the dish, they didn't show and were pretty indifferent about it.

Perhaps, I was overthinking their reactions and everyone was just focusing on their treats.

Mom got to cooking the foreign delicacy as she chit-chatted—an effort that soon sparked a heated, emotional argument.

"Kedu ihe ị chọrọ iji were Peppe?"[68] Nne demanded, voice trembling.

"Ka o wee gaa n'ihu n'agụ akwụkwọ ya na mba ọzọ. Anyị agafeela nke a, Nne. Ka anyị ghara

---

ịmalite ozo,"[69] Mom sighed, tossing the cooking spoon into the sink.

She stroked her forehead, shutting her eyes and taking several deep breaths.

"Nne," she began in a calm voice. "Ana m agbalị ime ka ụmụ m dịrị n'otu ma nye ha ndụ ka mma. Ejim ya n'aka dika nne ha."[70]

"Ọ bụ na mụ onwe m agaghị enwe ike ikwu ya? Azụlitela m nwa agbogho ahụ ka ọ bụrụ nke m kemgbe ụwa."[71]

The bickering of my mother and grandmother soon filtered into the living room, where we kids were watching TV. I suddenly felt conscious of the several pairs of eyes looking in my direction. Quietly, I got up and stalked to the kitchen.

"Peppe bụ anya m na ntị m. Amaghị m ihe m ga - eme ma ọ bụghị ya, ọkachasị ugbu a m na - alaghachi n obodo m,"[72] Nne lamented.

---

[69] "So that she can continue her education abroad. We have gone through this, Nne. Let's not start again."

[70] "Nne, I'm trying to unite my children and give them a better life. I want them with me."

[71] "So, I don't get a say? I have raised that child like my own."

[72] "Peppe is my eyes and ears. What will I do without her, especially now that

I heard the tears in her voice. It broke me to see my grandmother so vulnerable. I was used to seeing her as this strong character; it blinded me to the fact that she was human after all. We'd come this far together, and for the most part, I understood her sentiments. But Mom also had a point.

It sucked that I was the centre of attention, but no one cared enough to ask what I wanted. Above everything else, I wanted Nne to be happy. But I also wanted to be with my siblings and enjoy the warmth and love of my real birth mother. I hadn't even lived with the woman for an entire year, ever.

"Nne—"

Mom and her mother focused on me as I stepped into the kitchen.

"Gaghị anọ naanị gị n'obodo gị, ọ ga-enwe onye ga-egboro gị mkpa gị."[73]

The aged woman grabbed me and pulled me into a warm hug, crushing me to herself. I felt her tears on my clothes. I cried too.

"Nne, echegbula onwe gi. Aga m akpoku gi ugboro ugboro,"[74] I promised amidst sniffles.

I'm returning to the village?"

[73] "You won't be alone in the village. Someone will look after you."

"Nne, ndo. Ga-adị mma,"[75] Mom cut in, stooping to our level to join the hug-fest.

After several moments of whispered promises, we opened our eyes to see the rest of my siblings peering at us from the doorway, cheeky smiles dancing on their lips.

"Yabụ, ụnụ agaghị anabata nne nne gị?"[76] Nne queried, laughing.

***

Nne and the others soon cleared out of the kitchen, leaving me behind to help Mom serve the food. I returned from setting the table, which the others gladly occupied after watching me labour alone (*best siblings ever!*) to meet a strange sight.

"Mommy, look at the worms in this plate," I pointed at a serving of pasta mom had kept aside.

"Worms ke?" she sniggered. "Ngo, that is the pasta."

I refused to believe that a dish so elaborately named could have such a worrisome aesthetic. I bore

---

[74] "Nne, don't worry. I'll call regularly."
[75] "Nne, sorry. It's all right."
[76] "So, you guys won't come give your grandma a hug?"

the plates to the table with caution, holding them at arm's length should the "worms" decide to revolt, of course.

As soon as the plate kissed Bobo's table mat, he stabbed it with his fork, twisting and spooning a forkful of pasta into his mouth. His lips were coated in oil and he seemed to be enjoying the food.

So far, no worm had fought back.

When Nne got her serving, she studied it with scepticism.

"Kedu ihe bụ ihe a?"[77]

Laughter scattered across the table from my siblings. All except Mimi cared enough to chip in. My baby sister was having a field day keeping the noodles long enough on her plastic fork to get them in her mouth.

"Nne, it's spaghetti," Chidinma slurped a noodle, much to my disgust.

"Gini?"[78]

---

77 "What is this?"
78 "What?"

"Nne, ọ ga-amasị gị. Naanị nwalee ya,"[79] Mom interjected, entering the dining area with two bowls of steaming hot spaghetti, one of which she placed in front of an unoccupied seat for me.

I'd very much prefer not to eat this going forward, I pondered. My grandmother seemed to share my sentiments.

"Tah!"[80] Nne protested. "Biko, weta ofe ka m rie."[81]

Of Flights and Heavenly Places

"Don't take off the seatbelts or get out of your seats," Mom warned as she strapped us in.

The flight was preparing for take-off and passengers were mostly seated, all eyes fixed on the hostess presenting emergency safety procedures.

Nne had returned to the village the previous day, welcomed by the rest of her children. Mom had arranged for a help to cater for her. We got a chance to speak, and I reached out to my uncles, proudly declaring that I was going to the big city of London.

---

[79] "Nne, you'll like it. Give it a try."
[80] "Oh, please!"
[81] "Please, bring me soup instead."

What did they say about rejected stones again? I was elated.

The previous night, I could barely sleep and had been one of the first to wake up. We were out of the house in no time, leaving Uncle Chibuike to maintain mom's apartment. We managed to get out of the chronic Lagos traffic in time to make it for our flight.

Fortunately, I got a window seat, which fuelled both my anxiety and excitement. The air conditioning was on full blast, and I was cold to my core. No one else seemed to mind the winter we were experiencing; so, I had to adjust quickly.

As soon as the hostess completed her rendition, the passengers clapped her and the plane's door was shut. The hostesses took their places just behind the first-class cabin and radioed the pilot to take us away.

The plane taxied across the runway, pulling us back into our chairs as it gathered speed for lift-off. A tilt and a slow climb later and I lost my mind.

"Mommy, anyị na-arịgo!"[82]

---

[82] "Mommy, we'reg oing up!"

Mom forced a smile from her seat on the adjacent aisle, far from pleased by the attention I was attracting.

The plane settled in the atmosphere, stunning me into silence with the pleasant view of puffy clouds and shrunken geography.

When it was stable enough to move around, the hostesses got to serving the passengers. I was presented with a bowl of mashed potatoes, which I wrongly assumed was fufu.

The oddity tasted weird in my mouth, drawing a contorted look to my face. My siblings, with their much-experienced palate, were happily digging into their plates and conversing in low tones.

Dessert was served next, which astonished me to no small degree.

How much food did these people eat at once?

But even their dessert was no treat for my taste buds, which rejected them with a vengeance. I wound up eating only a fraction of my servings.

When the plates and trays were cleared away and put down respectively, the hostesses resumed their positions. My siblings drifted off to sleep soon afterwards, with Mom and I being the only ones awake.

"Mommy, anyị ga-aga eluigwe?"[83]

Mom looked in my direction, unable to contain her laughter.

"I ga-echere wee hụ."[84]

***

It was freezing when we arrived. Mom handed us jackets to put on before going out. We'd packed light for the trip, with mom promising to take us shopping there. So, there wasn't much luggage to share between us.

I was starstruck by London: the landscape, the weather, even the people.

"Mommy, lee ndi ocha!"[85] I pointed in glee. "Lee ndi Jesus."[86]

Mom was a little red in the face and withdrew my hand promptly, warning that it was rude to point. I was rooted to the spot taking in the view when my family started to exit the airport without me.

"Ngozi!"

---

[83] "Mommy, are we going to heaven?"
[84] "You'll have to wait and see."
[85] "Mommy, look at white people!"
[86] "Look at Jesus' people."

Mom's voice disrupted my reverie, bringing me back to the present. I hurried towards them. Soon we were on a bus headed for Mom's house.

The presence of more white people on the bus was another spectacle I relished until we alighted.

Mom's place was practically furnished with a touch of minimalism. It was considerably warmer than the outdoors. A heating system was responsible, Mom had explained when I asked.

For the next couple of days, we went and came in to acclimatize to the weather and get much-needed stuff, like groceries and clothes. I spent the bulk of my time hanging out in the lobby to catch sight of our white neighbours. When I wasn't being a silly creep, common sense prevailed and I marvelled at how far I'd come in some five-six years.

I'd gone from a village girl to a city girl to an even bigger city girl.

Ngozi to the world!

4

NEW WORLD, NEW PROBLEMS

The problem with moving to new places is that they hold new, sometimes unthinkable problems peculiar to the area. Relocating to the United Kingdom was the big break I'd expected for the bulk of my life, especially as a child growing up in the slums. The white man's land was a paradise far beyond my reach. The closest I'd gotten to it was in the movies about Jesus we used to see.

Some distance, you'd reckon.

The earliest part of my stay was spent noticing the many differences between the United Kingdom and Nigeria. Lagos used to be my pinnacle until I waltzed out of the airport doors of *ndi oyibo*. But even while being leagues above my country of descent, there were certain perks the UK lacked. For one, it was colder with overcast skies the bulk of the time. This meant we had to rely on heaters rather than sunlight for warmth and dress up in sweaters and jackets every other time we had to step out of the house.

It became a pretty tiring routine over time.

"Obodo a juru oyi!"[87] I complained to my mom several times.

"Ngo, it's the weather here," she'd shrug. "You'll get used to it."

The next challenge for me would be food. Their cuisines did nothing for my taste buds, and my once proudly protruding stomach had grown lean from picky eating. We got by on mashed potatoes and burgers, which seemed to be my siblings' favourite meals all of a sudden. Having given the weirdly coloured mash a try the last time, I thought

---

[87] "It's cold abroad."

I'd find solace in burgers. How badly could bread be prepared anyway?

Pretty badly, it turned out.

The idea not only struck me as odd but that I also had to deal with sauce racing along the contours of my hand and down my arm was no fun. Besides, who thought slapping bread onto fried minced meat was a good idea? That there are vegetables in it doesn't make it feasible still.

Thankfully, Mom brought along some ingredients for making *ofe oha*, which I had almost always until I'd completely depleted the stock.

It wasn't until a couple of months later that the school session began in the UK. Mom enrolled Chidinma and Bobo in secondary school and Mimi started kindergarten. Chioma and I stayed home for a little longer, much to my chagrin.

When Mom finally came round to enrolling me in school, she took me to a secondary school in the neighbourhood. The experience was no different from my first school in Lagos. We went in and I was drilled by an interviewer, a white man. However, unlike my primary school experience, I was better prepared now.

I answered his questions tactically and without hurry. He took down some notes as we spoke and tried to engage me in a conversation independent of academics. He nodded as we spoke, adjusting the tiny glasses hanging from his nose. His disposition gave nothing away as to how I performed, but I was confident in my answers and how I'd managed myself.

After the test, he met with Mom behind closed doors, where they discussed for some 20 to 40 minutes. When she emerged, Mom relayed the details of my evaluation without delay. The interviewer thought I'd done well and was a fairly bright child, but feared for my social and psychological development.

"Why?" I looked up at my mom, heart pounding.

"Because of the thing with your tongue."

"He doesn't like my accent?"

"No," mom shook her head. "Not that. I'm talking about this..." she gestured at her mouth.

"Oh," my face fell.

Sometimes, I forgot I had a cleft palate. Until there and then, I hadn't had a reason to feel bad about my condition in a while. In retrospect, it's pretty mind-boggling how I felt more comfortable back in Nigeria with a cleft palate than in the supposedly "saner clime" that was the United Kingdom.

"He said the kids might bully you for it."

My heart sank further.

In Nigeria, except for the times I looked in the mirror, or when unfortunate people went out of their way to point it out, I didn't feel overly conscious of my cleft palate. The other kids took me as I was and no one pointed out my condition, even if it stuck out like a sore thumb.

When we got back to the house, I broke down and cried.

Why does it have to be different every time? Why does everyone make objections that never go in my favour?

In my grief, my mind pondered the story of my birth. Mom had left me in the village because she couldn't deal with my condition, hadn't she? Had I not been abandoned, left with my grandparents because I was an eyesore? If my own mother could do that, I expected too much of others who didn't have anything to lose.

For the first time, I missed Nne. She wouldn't have understood, but it felt safe to cry to her and wail in her reassuring arms.

It didn't help that my siblings were making headway at their schools, while I was stuck waiting for some miracle to happen.

Luckily for me, Mom was on the lookout for different alternatives to save me from my grief. I was starting to shut out everyone as the days rolled by. My once bubbly personality had been reduced into a spectacle of self-loathing.

Now, the educational system in the United Kingdom differed from that back home. Here, one needed to go through primary school, secondary school, and college before one could attend a university. However, progression wasn't rigid after primary school; meaning, I could skip straight to college, but at the cost of spending two extra years in addition to the normal two-year duration. Also, college was tasking, because it determined whether or not you could attend a university.

I was 14 at the time and Mom thought I was better off at a college since the secondary school didn't work out, and sought to enrol me in a local one. While it was one less person to worry about for her, I was perturbed about attempting college without a strong educational background, especially as my academic development came rather late.

Secondary school lasted for six years, a duration I'd be skipping by jumping the gun. It scared me. Hearing about my cleft palate had ruined my confidence, so I couldn't put on a brave face. Nothing was brave about what I was about to do. If anything, I was being a reckless daredevil.

Neither my tears nor melancholy changed Mom's mind and soon, the enrolment was upon me.

When in Strange Places

I was admitted into Level One, which was some kind of O-Level (Ordinary Level) class that wrapped up secondary education and prepared students for the final two years of college or A-Level (Advanced Level). The fact that there were secondary school attendees at my level did nothing to alleviate my fears. Instead, I felt more on edge and uneasy.

College in the United Kingdom was no easy undertaking. We were treated as pseudo-university students and made to do lots of course work and exams, although the former took up the bulk of the school year. Mom had enrolled me in a course called GNVQ (General National Vocational Qualification) Studies in Business.

The course was alien to me and my inclination to business was non-existent. I was as ignorant as they come, with no idea of where to start from or what to do. But despite the pain of rejection, dwindling self-esteem, and mounting cluelessness, I was determined to excel at it.

If finishing college was all it took to end the nightmare, then so be it.

But life's no Disney movie and no halftime pep talk I'd encouraged myself with was going to work like magic. In fact, the minute I made up my mind to give my all, I ran into a wall. Learning English from second-language speakers was a far cry from being under the tutelage of native speakers. Accents flew over my head, and with it, meanings and understanding.

To pass the class, I had to comprehend what was being taught. But I couldn't. My writing was poor since I couldn't understand the lecturers enough to take notes. To make up for this apparent weakness and keep up with the volume of work doled out, I took to late-night studying. I soon got adept at it and sometimes stayed up until 4 a.m. burying my nose in textbooks and online libraries, and circling between my room and the dining area or living room. There simply was no place for lapses, especially as it'd been made clear that my condition was a disadvantage.

Another spanner in the wheel was confidence level, which, unsurprisingly, was at an all-time low. Because of this, I never felt at ease with what I'd learned and felt inadequate or ill-prepared almost always.

It takes a bit of confidence to pull off any academic task, especially as one can easily overthink and go the wrong way.

Personal studying came at a cost though. The longer I kept at it, the more I drifted apart from my siblings, growing into a bookworm who only lived to attend school and study. When I returned from college, I shut myself up in the room, only deigning to come out for meals. Replacing my once bubbly, smiling face was a hard, disillusioned look. In turn, my siblings grew estranged and kept to themselves, except for Chioma, who still managed to get some words out of me.

I felt that she understood me when she first reached out. But it turned out that Chioma was just as clueless as the others. Our conversations weren't anything beyond sibling squabbles and mindless hellos and bye. It drove me further into my shell.

But things didn't always continue in a downward spiral. I met a friend at school, Fiona, an Indian, whose fluency in English was just as delicate as mine. We bonded over our joint inability to comprehend the lecturers and began a great friendship that would outlast our troubled freshman year. With Fiona, it was easy to be me—a struggling student, doing her best to make decent grades. She understood me and saw through my facade faster than the rest of the class.

I suppose she might have first noticed me struggling to express myself around boys. *Fine girl like me*, I wasn't short of admirers who wanted to know my name for several reasons. And unlike Nigerians, it wasn't the weirdest thing in the world for strangers in the United Kingdom to ask for your name. With my history of gregariousness and talkativeness, one would imagine that I'd indulge them with my fierce exuberance.

But I didn't.

Every other time I had to express myself, the words of the interviewer played in my head like a broken cassette player caught in a loop. I became overly aware of my cleft palate and would mumble or pick my words, or straight-up avoid conversations.

"What's your name?" some rando would smile at me.

"Anna," I'd shoot back, walking away quickly or feigning busyness.

Never on God's green earth had I gone by the moniker *Anna*. But I wouldn't be caught dead telling them my real name. While the folks there excelled at their language, they were terrible at foreign languages and accents and totally butchered any name that wasn't mainstream to them. Meaning, I'd have to keep replying to help them pronounce *Ngozi* correctly, without making it sound like a Nigerian prince fresh off of a phishing scam.

Without Fiona in the picture, studies were the only thing keeping me grounded and focused. I wanted to prove the interviewer wrong at all costs.

Of Chances and Little Victories

"Would you like to go to the hospital and see if they can do anything about your condition?" Mom asked one day, frowning in concern.

She'd noticed the unusual quiet in the house when my siblings and I were together and how we all preferred to mind our companies. She'd studied me for a while before putting the pieces together.

The prospect that there could be a way out seemed appealing, but I wasn't entirely sold on the idea.

"No," I shot it down immediately, with no intention of dwelling on the subject any further.

It felt better when my condition faded into the background and all everyone saw was me. I didn't want to be a pity case with no identity outside of the condition. It seemed counterintuitive to turn down such a promising opportunity, but my mind was made up.

Days rolled by and I finished from Level One, acing the General National Vocational Qualifications in Business exams with merit. Level Two came around with a different twist: BTEC in Business Studies. The stakes were higher and the class was more tasking, but my attitude was unchanged. I was still a mysterious antisocial child with one friend, who seldom spoke to her siblings and stayed up all night to study.

It didn't come to me as a surprise that I was different; I'd known that all my life. But I wouldn't let people tell me what I could or couldn't achieve. The second course was due to last a year and included a GCSE (General Certificate of Secondary Education) exam, which was crucial to my progression to A-Level. The GCSE is to the United Kingdom what WASSCE is to Nigeria and West Africa.

I may not have been the keenest listener in class, and not for lack of trying. But I sure knew how to study hard. Before the exam, I'd completed and understood all six modules taught to my level. It was no surprise when the results came back with distinctions in all of them.

Having cleared the preliminary levels with exceptional grades, I was given the green light to proceed into advanced studies. I chose to pursue a BTEC certificate in Business Studies and A-Level in Financial studies. Never one to pass up on academic stress, I also enrolled for an English intensive class. I couldn't continue to rely on my after-school studies to help me all the way.

At some point, I'd have to deliver presentations and express myself in class. *What then? I couldn't shy from it forever.*

It helped that I'd grown my circle a little with new faces like Flavia, another foreigner, and a Nigerian called Tomi. Besides them, I'd become a little at ease and allowed for acquaintances: people I exchanged pleasantries with but wasn't very close to. Fiona was the closest of my friends though, and I owed her a great deal for building my confidence. My command of English was only fairly better than Fiona's, but she constantly came to me for help with the language.

It seemed insane that she'd entrust her growth to me, but I discovered over time that I grew faster with the responsibility of teaching her. Because of that, Fiona was my go-to study partner and associate. My mood got better as confidence surged and I started to be relatable again. The depression of not being enough was waning and for once, I felt whole. It'd been two years since my relocation to the United Kingdom, and I was only starting to truly settle in.

A-Level began and I took off at a frightening pace. If I studied hard in the previous years, I put in even more effort now. It didn't take long for my labours to pay off and my name was soon on the lips of teachers and blabbermouth students. I shot up the popularity charts on account of my academic performance and gained the attention of everyone who walked and breathed within the school. But my newfound fame could barely steer me off course.

It's not like I'd always been a gloomy shadow or couldn't handle fame. *I'm Peppe after all—the one and only.*

Another two years flew by in a blur and Advance Level was over. I graduated with three distinctions in BTEC; a solid B in A-Level Financial Studies; and a just-enough C in English to qualify me for the university.

Talk about going out with a bang!

The day I was handed the certificate was arguably the best day of my life. I thought I'd die from the joy. Tears cascaded down my cheeks as I pressed the hard-earned paper to my chest.

Finally, it was over now. All the hard work paid off.

Unto Newer Things

Forever the busybody, I started applying for universities with feverish determination, not sparing myself a few days off to bask in the glory of my accomplishments. Although my approach could be attributed to a never-say-die attitude, it was, in fact, that I wanted a change of environment.

College had provided me with a temporary distraction away from home, and I was glad for the chance to escape every other day. But, with those years out of the way, I felt myself sinking again, swallowed up by the choking bubble that was Birmingham. I'd never really settled into the city that was home to my family, and my guts churned at the thought of going to one of the local universities.

I wouldn't have my friends or reputation in the new environment, so I needed to make a decision that allowed me to breathe. I needed to keep my confidence level and academics stable to avoid the risk of depression.

With my certificate, I could apply to as many as five different universities for admission. If more than one of them accepted my proposal, I'd have to settle on a choice. All five of my applications were to universities outside of Birmingham, including Manchester and Bristol, and it baffled my mother to no small degree.

"Ngo, why do you want to leave Birmingham?" she queried, studying my application sheet. "There are some fine schools here."

"I know," I tried unsuccessfully to shrug her off.

But Mom was one persistent woman.

"Ngo, you can't study outside of Birmingham. What's the point going so far out anyway?"

I couldn't bring myself to tell her about the ordeals of being in a place I was most uneasy.

"The schools here don't have what I want to study."

It broke my heart to lie to her, but there was no other way. Mom wouldn't back off if she knew my reasons, and she sure wouldn't have understood them either.

But all the pressure surrounding my decision to school elsewhere soon blew over when I received several return letters. About four universities had written back offering me admission, and it was up to me to decide which of them was best suited. My circle outside of Birmingham was limited, and the only one friend, a girl, I had in the five locations I applied for resided in Bristol. But I didn't have the longest relationship with this girl, and our friendship didn't run that deep. So, she wasn't enough reason for me to want to change location.

But it was better than being a total stranger in a new place; so, I accepted the offer from The University of the West of England, Bristol to study Business and Financial Accounting. I received some forms, which I filled out and returned promptly. With the paperwork out of the way, I was due to resume in September, 2010.

Leading up to the time of my departure, I still embodied my antisocial ways: steering clear of in-house dramas and sibling rivalries. I desperately wanted to have fun again and mess around with my siblings, but the desire to prove the interviewer wrong trumped my wish to connect. I also needed to prove to myself that there was more to me than others had seen or assessed me by.

Of course, I had the little victories to show. But all that success had been born from a place of sorrow and pain of being different. All along, I'd carried myself proudly, masking the low self-esteem and lack of confidence that gnawed at my sanity, driving me barmy.

In my quest for solace, I'd become a loner, which was the worst possible tag I could've brought on myself.

"You must be a witch," Chioma had said once, scrunching her face. "Otherwise, why are you always on your own? Or, do you think you're better than us since you're in a bigger school?"

It amused me how I could be branded as the ill-fitting one by people who barely knew or felt my pains. I had to live every day knowing I was different with a condition that set me apart from others, and not in a good way.

"You wouldn't get it," I sighed, shaking my head, sadness evident in my tone. "None of you do."

5

A HOME AWAY FROM HOME

Mom and I set out to Bristol sometime in September. School was due to resume in another nine days, and I wanted to settle in and get used to the environment to avoid the rush on resumption day. Mom helped me pack, while my siblings loaded my stuff into the boot. For each luggage moved, my room grew more generic until it was just bare walls and aged papers from my college days.

My mind was agog with thoughts of what university might be like—a ploy to avoid the thought of leaving home, and the overwhelming anxiety that came with such big decisions. I'd been putting off the thought for days now, surprised by how harder it was to actually leave. I thought I was finally done with Birmingham and needed the time away from my family, but I began missing them days before I even stepped out of the door.

"Go wait in the car," mom entered the room. "I'll be with you shortly."

I sighed quietly, shoulders slumped and gave my room a final glance. The bedding had been undone and folded into a neat pile on the mattress, which laid bare in its stand. The piles of books that once adorned the tiny, overhanging shelf had been cleared out: the important ones stuffed away with the rest of my stuff and the others put into a cardboard box to be donated to the local library.

My siblings and I shared a moment of quiet goodbyes and they took turns hugging me. I chewed on my lips, intent on holding back the tears that threatened to fall.

Mom joined me in the car after a bit and we hit the open road. The rain had let up slightly and the sun peered through the grey September sky. The over two-hour drive to Bristol was relatively quiet. Mom played the radio at a reasonable volume and bobbed to the music, while I pillowed my head on an arm and stared blankly at the whizzing landscape.

Mom stole several glances at me, but said nothing to ease my mind or inquire about my countenance. My head had quieted a little during the journey, but my heart rate was still outrunning Wile E. Coyote. Encouraged by the lack of conversation, I drifted asleep to R.E.M.'s Everybody Hurts.

The next time I opened my eyes, Mom had parked the vehicle in a compound and alighted.

"Ngo," she pulled back the door of the passenger seat, jolting me. "We're here."

Two Chelsea boots-clad feet kissed the drenched grounds of the dormitory, and an inquisitive pair of eyes peeked out of the car. I shut the door and studied the place I'd be staying for the session. Mom led the way inside to a reception, where I confirmed my details and picked up a key and room number.

My lodge was a four-bedroom apartment complete with a large bathroom, kitchen, and balcony that opened out to the road leading towards the university. Mom and I set my things down and did some unpacking. The rooms had been cleaned to perfection and readied for occupancy, so it helped with speed. After doing some light arrangements, it was time for Mom to go. The much-dreaded period was upon us.

"Ngo, I'll take my leave now," she stepped towards me and placed a hand on my head.

I expected words of encouragement but looked up to see her eyes shut and her head bowed in prayers. I lowered my head and said my Amens. After the prayers, Mom announced her departure again, but reluctantly this time. She fiddled with her purse to hide the fact she was dragging her feet.

Burying my face into her shoulders, I hugged her tightly, feeling the tears burn down my cheeks.

"Mommy, can I return with you until school actually resumes? I've already moved in so it'll be much easier when the time comes."

She smiled, patting my back.

"Ngo…"

"I'll come back on my own, I promise," my words were muffled by sniffles.

The realization that I was all by myself in a strange land hit harder than I expected. Sure, Bristol was only some two hours away, but with my soon-to-be busy schedule and Mom's, we'd barely have the chance for regular visits.

The only friendly face I knew around town resided with her family in Bristol. But even she lived quite the distance from my apartment, and relying on her to show me around was going to be tasking. I didn't have a car or a year-round bus pass, so it would be expensive to make that many trips.

Either Mom agreed with my sentiments or was hesitant about leaving her baby in a new place, but I was back home the same day.

The next time I touched down at Bristol on the eve of resumption, I met three other students, who would be my flatmates for the school year. Unsurprisingly, I was the only black person among them. But that didn't stop us from getting to know each other. Dare I say that none of them saw me as a person of colour, and I was accorded equal respect. In fact, I expected my flatmates would be prim and proper until they dragged me along to a nightclub.

Since coming to the United Kingdom, I'd been the ideal child: only ever going to school or church. Otherwise, I was home the rest of the time. It didn't help that Birmingham had a curfew that prevented any form of night-time activities. Not that it bothered me though. But here I was in my first weekend at the university, and I was already willing to party like it was '99.

Mom would've had a heart attack.

I got to the club not knowing what to expect but got more than I bargained for. The music was all kinds of confusing; the disk jockey more so.

How did folks enjoy British music when it sounded so wrong?

Suffice it to say: clubbing is just a loud room with equally loud people. Uneasiness washed over me as I stood against a wall timidly while my flatmates writhed and twirled to the rhythm of the music. I craved the comfort and warmth of my bed, despising the cold, thick air of the club, which smelled of smoke and drinks, driving me barmy. But I couldn't bring myself to make my flatmates abandon their night out. In fact, I believed they all thought I was out there having fun as well.

I glanced at my watch. It was barely an hour since we arrived. I could've sworn it was longer.

Slowly, the music started to get to me, and I was soon on the dancefloor busting out moves with the gang.

Who'd have thought!

It wasn't until 4 a.m. that the nightmarish turned great outing ended, and we returned to the apartment. We were out as a light in no time, snoring as soon as our heads touched the pillow.

***

School resumed in earnest and with it my aversion to socializing. I spent more time in the library and behind the doors of my room, buried in piles of books and assignments. My social circle had suffered as a result and I'd only made one friend. Duna was way older than me, with something of a 15-year gap or thereabouts. But she was smart and fun to be with in the way that geeks could be.

She was a bookworm herself, who I'd first noticed on the second week of coming to the library. Duna was almost always in the Level Three Library, in the same spot next to the large window. Another constant was a pair of earphones she regularly sported, bobbing to music as she read.

If that wasn't the most attractive thing in the world to my young mind!

We'd become friends shortly afterwards, and I was more than satisfied to leave my circle at that. Besides, Duna was in all my classes and we were studying for the same major. It was a match orchestrated by the book gods.

Duna couldn't have come at a more pristine time. She kept me grounded and helped to channel my focus in the fast-paced, distracting world that was the university. It was only my first night when I went clubbing and had my first experience of alcohol. My desire to grind out results may be unyielding, but I was still quite naive and prone to succumbing to peer pressure.

But with Duna around, that part of me rescinded. I'd become a shadow, following her to the library or the quiet fields to study. Nothing else mattered.

Or did it…?

Heavy Lies the Head

Tertiary education in the United Kingdom was a whole different ball game. Here, the government covered tuition until one graduated and got a job. Think of it as the Student Loan scheme of America, but better.

Since relocating to and schooling in the U.K., I had to apply for permanent residency, which wasn't completed until the 1st of September, mere weeks from when school resumed. The timing couldn't have been better. Armed with this new sense of pride, I'd gone on to school.

I mean, the Crown paid my tuition. What else could be greater than that?

Three months into the semester, I got a letter from the government. As my eyes perused the lines, my heartbeat grew louder and tears welled in my eyes.

I wasn't eligible for the scheme because my permanent residency was a little too late.

Why could nothing go right for me in education?

I pondered the likelihood of dropping out and returning home. I thought about Mom and how much she must be dealing with managing so many kids as a single parent. It'd be wicked of me to return home and pile more misery on her already ladened shoulders.

Duna came in with some handy advice and helped me appeal to the office in charge of the Student Finance scheme. I appeared before several officials and pleaded my case with steely determination.

At the time, I was living relatively poor. After the first month's rent that Mom had covered for me, she could do no more. The government was supposed to cover both tuition and living expenses. But since repealing my eligibility, I was two months behind on rent and on the verge of being kicked out of school.

For the few months I was in school, I lived off of handouts from my flatmates and the meagre

£20 to £30 Mom sent my way every other fortnight. Something had to give, and fast.

"Hmmm," the official fingered his stubbled chin. "This is one peculiar case."

I sat across from him, pulling a brave face, whilst praying that he would give me a scintilla of hope. Anything to give me a fighting chance, however slightly. The official was the last one willing to interview me, with the others claiming nothing could be done about my case.

"The problem here lies in the resumption date of your school and not the timing of your residency," he leafed through my file. "No one could have predicted that."

Silence.

I wrung my hands.

So far, this was the most interest I'd gathered since starting the appeal. But I was afraid of hoping for anything. It'd be much better to give up now than to have my hopes crushed. I couldn't live with the heartbreak.

"See," he dropped the file on the broad, oak table and turned it my way, "if your residency had come in on the second, then there is nothing we can do. But since it came a day earlier, there is a bit of a grey area we can work around."

"D-does that mean I won't get kicked out of school?" I swallowed hard, my voice rising slightly.

"I think so. You leave the administrative parts to me and go on with your school work. I'll ensure you get your eligibility and the benefits that come with it."

If it wasn't unprofessional, I'd have hugged this balding, fifty-something year old and cried on his shoulder.

I left the office feeling lighter, with a spring in my step.

But it wasn't all roses and sunflowers afterwards. Student Finance still had to process my eligibility and work around some bureaucracies before I could get any money. But I had to live long enough to see that happen, and for that, I needed food and transport fare and a house over my head. I couldn't rely on handouts forever. Besides, who'd willingly give me my rent?

I considered getting a part-time job to supplement my miserable finances and applied to several places around the neighbourhood. My credentials spoke for me and I got a call up for the role of a sales assistant during the weekends. The gig offered amazing flexibility that could offer me more hours within the week, so long as I requested overtime beforehand.

Naturally, I shouldn't have to work, having only been in the university for less than a quarter. I was trying to play God in a series of events whose outcomes were as unknown as they could be devastating. But I couldn't just sit still and hope for things to become right. I had to do something. So, much to Duna's chagrin and common sense, I accepted the job.

Work started in full swing in November, and I was given four hours for the entire weekend. It seemed too little considering the state I was in, so I spoke with my boss and requested more hours. Granted, I worked 12 hours on Saturdays and Sundays, and more hours during the week, when I didn't have lectures.

Duna was a lovely friend through my dark patches. To ensure I didn't lag behind at school, she ensured I devoted some time to study in the library. She'd swing by my workplace in her car and drive us both to libraries within and outside the university. She was like the school mother I never had.

Alternating between work and school was tough. I couldn't even pretend to be having a it good, because I was winded most of the time. My schedule was at breaking point, but I couldn't quit or wallow in self-pity. I wasn't as privileged as the others, nor did I have anything to return to if I failed to continue.

It didn't help that school was tasking in and of itself. It was nothing like college. Here, your writing needed to follow a prescribed pattern, and I'd never had the best fluency in written or spoken English.

On The Wings of Time

It wasn't until Student Finance cleared me that I learned to breathe again. With tuition secured for the rest of my university days, my foot came down hard on the gas. Freshman year flew by in a breeze and I aced my courses. The second-year was more or less the same: distinctions and Bs all the way. Then the third year came around—the most intensive of them all. The make-or-break moment. There were dissertations to write and presentations to make. It was no time to be distracted. But even that was beneath me; I passed gracefully.

All through the years, I kept my job as a sales assistant and had come to love it. The chance to break away from the university scenery for a bit and put all I'd learned to use had grown from a necessary evil to a hobby. Now, I was just being paid to do what I loved best: manipulate figures.

Besides enjoying my work, I was in it for the money too. I still had to feed, clothe, and transport myself every now and then. I also needed to save up and apply for British citizenship. It wasn't enough to have a residency permit, as it further limited my already narrow range of opportunities.

Now, I was fully responsible for myself and had stopped relying heavily on my mom. The once shy, reserved girl had blossomed into a social, pseudo-independent woman who bossed school and work-life balance with mind-blowing precision.

I'd even gone as far as having a boyfriend and chucking my v-card onto the growing pile of girls who'd done it in university. But with first-time intimacies came first heartbreaks, and even that didn't elude me. Not that it posed an inhibition. In fact, it was quite the contrary.

Sure, I cried about it and moaned to whoever cared to listen for days. But as soon as I was over it, there was no turning back.

My confidence level was at an all-time high and I breezed through social situations like a veteran model through a runway of spectators.

***

I turned 21 just after the first year, and I couldn't have been prouder of my accomplishments. Some 13 years ago, I was just another girl child living it out in the slums with no identity or idea of what the future held.

Friends turned up to my apartment bearing gifts and whatnot. My flatmates were being their cheerful selves and planning a little get-together with the small crowd that was starting to amass. Then showed up a friend of mine, Debby, who handed me the strangest gift ever.

"Happy birthday, Angie!" she pressed a small bible into my hand. "Many happy returns."

Now, I was Christian and considered myself to be quite devout. Having been raised catholic by my grandparents, I said my prayers to the rosary fairly regularly and kept lent when I remembered. But I'd never needed to own a bible because it just wasn't necessary. The Father did the reading anyway, and the passages were projected for all to see. Beyond the tiny leaflets and circulars passed around to members, I'd never seen the need to delve deeper, let alone get around to studying the Bible.

"Uh… thanks…?" I thumbed the blue hardback, sizing up the volume.

I was slightly weirded out and disappointed by the present. I mean, anyone would prefer something fanciful for their 21st, not something as grave as a bible.

Sheesh!

But Debby wasn't done. Next, she was dragging me along to one of the local Pentecostal churches: Christ Embassy. I went in grudgingly and went on to have the time of my life. The experience was surreal. When the service was over, I was born again. Not that I never believed in God or had strayed from my Catholic ways. But this time, I felt Him closer. Like I could tell him things in ways I never did. I was coming to the realization that God loved and wanted the best for me.

I'd go on to start studying the Bible Debby gifted me and learned to rely and call on God for help. I had strived to build my physical life throughout the years. Perhaps, it was time to do the same for my spiritual one.

Bye-bye, Bristol

By the turn of my last year in university, I turned in my dissertation and sat for the final exams. The results were out in June; I'd graduated with a second class upper. I cried and laughed all at once, pressing the result to my chest.

I reached for my phone to tell Mom the great news.

"I did it, mommy! I did it!"

"Ngo?" Mom was alarmed. "What did you do?"

"The results are out. I made a 2.1"

Mom screamed on the other end of the line, forcing me to back away from the phone. I heard her burst into songs and pictured her doing a little dance around the apartment.

"Oh, chi'm! My own Ngo is now a graduate!"

When her excitement had died out a bit, we spoke at length about our respective ends' goings-on. Mom started to sing again as I hung up.

I laid in bed staring at the ceiling, recalling all the struggles and pains that went into the process that birthed the present. For lack of better grammar, I'd wound up with a second class. Regardless of how punctual I was to classes and how much time and effort I devoted to my assignments, that problem lingered, stifling my creativity.

But, boy, was I glad to have triumphed above all odds!

Graduation day came the following month, and it was an emotional one. My family came in from Birmingham with some other relatives that were visiting the country. It'd been years since we all met like that.

The event got underway and I sat with the rest of my class, all garbed in gowns and hats, waiting for the roll call. I trembled slightly when my name was called and took several breaths to calm myself to no avail. I walked up the podium with heavy, unfeeling feet and shook hands with the vice-chancellor while posing for the photographer.

The light flashed, catching the tears that had started to stream down my face, ruining my makeup.

It was all inexplicable how I'd come this far. Here I was, a girl with no secondary school education, being presented with a degree by a prestigious academic.

It made no sense!

I knew several classmates who were repeating a year—most of them British by birth, with great elementary and secondary educational history.

On one hand, I wanted to jump and scream and run around with reckless abandon. On the other hand, I wanted to collapse in a heap and have a good cry. I caught Mom drying tears from the corners of her eyes. My siblings perused the event dry-eyed.

I chuckled, making a mental note of my achievements:

Angie Ngozi, 23, British citizen, Second Class degree holder (Business and Financial Accounting).

That sounded about right.

By working overtime and practising extreme savings, I'd managed to save up enough to apply for and get British citizenship. It didn't come cheap though and took a lot of courage to not postpone it for the future. I had to work overtime during the holidays while my mates were out vacationing and shopping for the new semester or session. It's a miracle I didn't feel pressured and kept my cool.

The memories brought a smile to my face. I breathed in the cool, morning air still heavy with the smell of greenery covered in dew. Fulfilment rang in my ears.

I was ready to take on the world!

6

BACK TO BIRMINGHAM

After my graduation, I moved back to Birmingham to live with my mom and siblings. The relocation wasn't as much my choice as it was obligatory at the time. I still had my part-time job as a sales assistant and could easily have asked Human Resources for full-time employment until I was settled in enough to begin writing applications again.

But I had a different gut feeling and couldn't quite bring myself to stay at the job any longer. It didn't help that some of my colleagues were also graduates who'd stayed for longer but never got round to seeking greener pastures elsewhere.

The job just didn't allow for the freedom necessary to write and mail applications or attend interviews. Work began in earnest by 9 a.m., but workers had to come in about an hour earlier. So, the only way to get a new job was to quit. But that was risky, especially as applications may not always pay off.

Deciding to leave was by far my biggest decision yet. I was broke and in need of all the money I could get; all my savings and disposable income had gone into getting my British passport.

Leaving the oddly comfortable life of an independent young adult to move back in with my mom wasn't the ideal scenario I would have wanted. But I wasn't about to let it get to me. I decided my credentials were inviting enough to get me out of the house and on my feet in about a month or two. It helped that I was no longer constrained by school and could set my sights on anywhere I so pleased. There were no limits. I felt elated.

If only!

Three months flew by in a haze and with it the chances of getting responses from the applications I sent out. I was still unemployed and living by the rules of my mother. I redid my resume and chucked in bits of qualifications and skills to bolster its appeal. It didn't matter that I didn't have any of the newfound skills or credentials. Desperation was high and I was just about going mad with anxiety already.

By the fourth month, I got my first glimmer of hope. Some of my applications were replied to and I was scheduled for several interviews across the month. It felt good to be acknowledged.

But the unemployed life wasn't quite done with me. Even after pulling stellar performances at interviews and travelling long distances to attend, I was turned down based on my lack of experience. I put up a brave face for a while to avoid buckling under the weight of each crippling rejection.

Money was also running out, and I soon had to trigger the student overdraft clause I'd particularly left untouched throughout my years at the university. I got a loan of £1,500, which I used to finance my travels to attend interviews and send applications. Even worse, since I'd sent my resume far and wide, I had to make expensive trips via rail—all of which cut deeply into my already beggared finances.

"I'm afraid you're not what we are looking for at this time."

"I'm so sorry, but we are interested in someone who is more experienced."

Rejections flew in as fast as I returned from the trips. No one was willing to take a gamble on a fresh undergraduate. It soon started to get to me and my rock steady resolve gave in. Confidence level plummeted, and with it, the zeal to continue.

Had I come this far only to be rejected on the grounds of inexperience?

The overdraft had been exhausted and I was worse off than when I first began. I couldn't turn to my mother for financial help. It was enough trouble moving back in with her, it'd be unhelpful to become more of a financial constraint.

To Mom, my job search was going well, what with the many different interviews I'd attended. It was only a matter of time before I was called to start. I did nothing to change this erroneous narrative for fear of how she'd react. My bank balance was in the negative and I couldn't even afford staples like sanitary pads and whatnot. I had to improvise and use tissue paper as a makeshift tampon cum pantyliner.

Six months into unemployment, I started applying for jobs more out of frustration than intent. With no money left to fund my expensive but futile interview trips and the stubbornness to avoid getting my mom involved, I decided to write to the local government.

I conveyed my deplorable living conditions and the length of my unemployment. Fortunately, they heeded and placed me on a scheme that paid about £20 to £30 per week. This was a meagre sum that could barely afford bus passes or train tickets, talk less of living expenses. But it was better than the nothing I'd earned in the last half a year since graduation.

In an unexpected twist of fate, the government decided to foot my interview bills for a definite period, given that I was willing to work. It seemed like I'd happened on the finest piece of luck.

But it came at somewhat of a demeaning cost.

Every other week, I had to go down to the local government secretariat to journal how my job search was going and how I was managing the funding. This responsibility sickened me. It felt like I was going to be served handouts and made to answer to the powers that be because they now had shares in my personal affairs.

Worst of all, the people who benefited from the same scheme were nothing like me. They were mostly hobos, street urchins, and drug abusers living off of government funding, not smart, intelligent graduates like me. It was embarrassing to be seen with that lot.

The only thing greater than the embarrassment was the depression that developed over time. I was struggling to ground myself and would sometimes space out from overthinking. Depression got me waking up early, doing chores around the house, bathing, and heading out like I had a job. The facade was good enough to fool my family and friends, save Chidinma and Ola, a friend I'd bonded with over the troubles of life. I needed someone to talk to before I went mad with worry, and I'd confided in her.

Ola encouraged me to the best of her ability, and her words were, sometimes, the only thing that got me through the day.

Of Heavy Hearts and Pleas of Death

As humans, we learn to adapt to situations, thrive in them, or give in. Over eight months of unemployment got me through all three stages. I'd had it up to here and prayed that God would take my life.

What else was there to live for? I'd grown up struggling to find my way after the demise of my grandfather. Relocating to Lagos brought its fair share of educational setbacks, as was moving to the United Kingdom. Now, even after graduation, I couldn't land a decent gig to sustain myself. It seemed like my life was one long tale about suffering.

The least I could do was die and ease the financial burden on my mother. If I can't be useful to her alive, hopefully, my death could mean something.

At this point, I lost weight rapidly and looked like a shadow of myself. My eyes were red from crying too much, and bags and dark circles presented from sleeplessness.

Chidinma was an absolute angel, forwarding me some £10 to £20 when she could. I felt terrible accepting the help because she was at the university and needed all the money she could get. It'd be harrowing for me to depend on my younger sibling and her petty income, especially as she was dipping into her allowance from home.

By the ninth month, I was all but tired of being turned down. I'd roamed many parts of the country at this point: Brighton, Birmingham, Bradford, Essex, London, Norwich, Manchester, among others. Like it wasn't bad enough that I was broke, my jacket was stolen at an interview in Manchester when I went to have a wee.

Just brilliant!

I could have died from frostbite that day. The weather was anything but hot, and being caught outside in thin, worn clothes was no way to survive the return trip from the swanky Manchester side.

This experience was the last line of hope for me. I'd just about toured an entire country in search of a job. Surely, I had to start thinking outside the box if I wanted to die with some food in my belly at the very least. Devastated and without options, I lowered my standards and began applying for the role of a sales assistant. I'd landed the gig in my undergraduate years, after all. Perhaps, the goal is to start small, build enough experience, then go big. How hard could it be!

A lot harder, it turned out.

I received return emails stating, "You don't have enough experience for the role." Or, "We apologize, but you are unqualified for this position."

Dear God! What else could they possibly need?

My sense of pride was all but gone, so I reconciled my anger and tried again. This time, for even smaller ventures. I applied as a shop assistant at local businesses, but each one had one reason or the other why they couldn't employ me.

The lower I fell, the higher desperation soared. At some point, I applied to accounting firms for apprenticeship and free labour. Anything to get me out of the house and restore my sense of competence. I hated that I was flailing helplessly. Surprisingly, even that got shot down.

Suffice it to say, that was the final straw that broke the camel's back.

Gone, Gone, the Form of Man...

Mom had gone to work as usual and the rest of my siblings were out at their respective places of studies. I was alone at home with nothing for company save a few ill-fated thoughts. I secured the door locks and settled within myself that I was on the right path.

I had to be sure. It wouldn't help to change my mind halfway when it was already too late.

For one who was about to take her own life, I was pretty pristine about it. I prayed for a bit, listened to some gospel songs, and read the bible.

You know, typical suicide pre-tasks.

I'd spent the past few years claiming God's blessings and promises. But if he had heard me, he didn't show. *Because why else was he watching me suffer?*

I grabbed my laptop and connected to the apartment Wi-Fi. After a few clicks and taps, I was online. My hands danced across the keyboard, entering a query:

How to commit suicide…

I reached for the enter button but withdrew long enough to enter some more characters.

…painlessly.

I'd been through enough pains already. No need to bring more upon myself, innit?

I don't know if I expected I was the only one suffering or with the worst luck, but I certainly wasn't expecting the tons of results I got. In fact, I happened on a website with specifically curated tips on how to commit suicide. Curiosity got the better of me and I got engrossed in the comments, where I found many people going through worse conditions than mine.

Unemployment was weighing me down when people out there were having the rottenest luck.

For the next hour and a half, I was going through the stories of people who wanted to commit suicide and had attempted, failed, and want to try again.

It seemed like one big clubhouse of the mentally unstable, I was too scared to proceed any further with my intentions.

Shouldn't there be some sort of natural mechanism that prevented people from harming themselves, I pondered.

One of the most shocking stories I came across was from a rando, a guy, who claimed that the easiest, most painless way to die was by ingesting poisonous liquids. He assented to have tried it once and was on the verge of death until his "stupid mother" happened on him fighting for life and called emergency services.

"Now, I'm back to living in this dump with her in a body I hate and a life I don't want," he wrote. "You all out there reading this. Ensure that no one barges in on you before you die. It ruins everything. 10/10 will try again. See you never."

I'd seen enough to nauseate me. Shutting the laptop, I hogged the bedspread and slipped into a moment of sombre reflection. In a way, I wasn't entirely unemployed by chance. Earlier in my job search, Mom had tried convincing me to come work with her. She worked in the health industry as a carer for the elderly. The pay was decent and she seemed to be doing well for herself. But I'd never imagined myself dealing with seniors, never mind actually taking it up as a job.

I had no passion for health or caregiving and would sooner succumb to my suicidal inclination than ply Mom's trade with half-hearted efforts. But with the way things had panned out, I started to rethink the offer. Had Mom insisted again, I just might have given in.

A Glimmer of Hope…?

A couple of days after my fickle attempt at suicide, I got a mail from the NHS (National Health Service), inviting me for an interview early the next day. I didn't think much of it because the NHS had sent me lots of similar emails in the past. The interview was slated to be held in Devon, somewhere around the South Coast of the country.

I rolled my eyes at the location, making a mental note of how much I had at hand and whether or not the interview was worth attending. In the end, I decided to give it a shot and began making arrangements accordingly. I woke early the next day and had a hurried bath before ringing the local taxi company to schedule a pickup by 5 a.m.

A honk announced the arrival of my ride a few minutes later. I stepped out of the house to meet the driver, an aged fellow with streaks of silver hair scattered across his balding head.

"Mornin', missy!" he sounded cheerful, helping me into the back of the cab before resuming his place behind the wheel.

"Where are we headed?" he keyed the ignition and twisted. The engine spluttered to life.

"Devon."

The key turned anticlockwise and the engine was silent again. The driver spun around in his seat.

"Ma'am, did you say *Devon*?"

I nodded before realizing my error.

"I beg your pardon, sir. I'm headed for the train station, where I'd catch the tube to Devon."

I imagined how much of a surprise it must have been for him. It was probably his first trip for the day and I was already planning a cross-country adventure.

"That's one long trip down South!" he whistled, turning around to start the car. "Anything special happening in Devon?"

"Not that I know of," I muttered. "I'm attending an interview."

"Would you look at that!" he adjusted the rear-view mirror, catching my gaze. "Hardworking as they come, eh? That's commendable—that you are defying the distance and willing to work."

I smiled sadly. *If only he knew.*

We drove for a few minutes before he spoke again.

"Would you take it?"

"Pardon?" I straightened from the windowpane I'd rested my head, staring into the rear mirror.

This time, however, he didn't look. Instead, focusing on the road ahead, which was starting to light up with all the colours of dawn.

"The job. If you got it, would you take it?"

A sigh escaped my lips followed by some moments of tensed silence. I composed myself and told him my story.

He was sympathetic and wished me well. We even shared a prayer, in which he implored that I got everything I desired.

As he prayed, I cried quietly in the back, overwhelmed by the fact that a total stranger was concerned enough about my plight to wish me well. I couldn't have wished for a better start to the day.

"You keep giving it your best shot, missy," he advised, scratching his beard. "It's not very rosy for people of colour in this climate."

I said my bye at the train station and boarded the over five-hour tube to Devon. The interview was fairly uneventful in itself, and when I was done, it was raining heavily. I couldn't imagine waiting out the rain for fear that it might continue the entire day.

Really peculiar weather the U.K. has.

It didn't help that I couldn't afford to hail a cab to take me back to the train station at Devon, so I decided to take my chances with the rain. I stepped out of the hospital and began the long trek.

Rain pelted down on my head, shoulders, and back as I walked, drenching me. The situation and weather were perfect, so I had a good cry as I went.

I couldn't have gone 10 minutes when my phone beeped quietly, drowned out by the loud pitter-patter of rain in my ears. I felt a slight tremor in my bag and felt inside for my phone. Cupping a hand around the screen, I flicked down the notification panel and caught the notification. It was from the NHS.

I brushed tears away with the sleeve of my coat and proceeded to open the message:

Unfortunately, you are not what we are looking for at this time...

They couldn't even wait to give me the bad news. Wow!

Fresh tears brimmed in my eyes, temporarily blurring the content of the mail. I fell to my knees, my body quaking with sobs.

It took a while to collect myself and continue the long walk to the station. It was still raining when I arrived and boarded the return tube. With the AC running, I was freezing in my drenched clothes—my teeth chattering uncontrollably.

I pondered the almost six-hour journey back home, including a stop at Bristol before continuing back to the Birmingham station, where I still had to walk to the bus stop to catch a bus heading for my mother's. It was enough hard work not bursting into tears for all to see.

When I got home, I confined myself to the room and mourned the waste of a long day. To think I'd grown hopeful and looked forward to the interview after my encounter with the driver that morning.

At Road's End

If my wit's end had a wit's end, I was there by the tenth month of unemployment. I didn't want to give up hope, but I also didn't want to prime myself for nothing. At this point, I couldn't care less about what job I could land. Even if it paid in cereal, I'd gladly sign my name in blood.

One rainy morning, after another semi-sleepless night of crying and overthinking, my phone buzzed to life. I eyed it from the bed, unwilling to make the effort to move. The ringing seemed to continue forever and it was starting to become infuriating.

I rolled over and snatched the device from the bedside table. It was an unknown number. I punched green.

"Hello, am I unto Angie Ngozi?"

"Yes," I stressed my reply, frowning slightly. I couldn't recognize the voice.

"Very well. I'm Emma from Adecco. I found your CV online; very impressive, I must say."

I sat up straight, my heart thumping loudly.

"Thank you…?"

"Well, I have a job for you, Angie. Just to be clear, you're in Bristol, right?"

"Why, of course!" I slipped out of bed, stepping into my slippers.

A lie, apparently. But I couldn't risk being turned down on the basis of being in the wrong city.

"Great. So, Angie, the job I have for you concerns payrolls. Basically, a payroll manager in a nursing home. We are short-staffed at the moment and need someone with your credentials for immediate employment."

I tried to speak but words failed me. Too dazed to speak or move, with my phone pressed against my ears, I listened to Emma ramble on about the position.

"How soon can you come in so I can brief you more—"

"Tomorrow!" I blurted out, suddenly finding my voice.

"Love the enthusiasm," Emma added, surprise etched in her voice.

"I beg your pardon. I'll be there bright and early tomorrow. I just need to tidy a few things and clear my schedule."

"I understand. See you then, Angie. Bye for now."

With that, she hung up.

Suddenly finding my pace, I made a beeline for my wardrobe and began hurriedly packing my stuff into an overnight case. My mind was already fixed on going to Bristol the same day. However, I had nowhere to stay and no money to afford accommodation, but I didn't let that get to me just yet.

I had a quick bath and brushed my teeth. For the first time in ages, I felt thrilled by the prospect of something going in my favour. I couldn't even muster the appetite to eat. I just wanted to be in Bristol quickly. Grabbing my phone, I went through my contacts, vaguely recalling some friends from university days who lived there or thereabouts. Luckily, I found one, Daniel Carr, a Briton, who resided in Bristol with a couple of friends in a shared apartment. The house had four independent bedrooms, with each occupant having one to himself.

I rang him.

"Hey, Daniel. Umm… this is going to sound weird because we haven't kept in touch much since uni, but do you mind if I crash at yours for a bit?"

"Are you kidding? Sure."

"Just like that?" I put the phone away from my ear to be sure I was on to the right recipient.

"Yeah, why?"

"No. Never mind. Thanks, man. I won't inconvenience you at all. In fact, I'mma sleep on the floor or the couch if I have to. I just need to be in Bristol for an interview."

"Enough talk, Angie. I got you. Come on over."

The whole conversation seemed scripted, and I was a little surprised at how everything was going well.

With accommodation sorted, I picked my stuff and headed out, ringing Mom on my way to the bus stop. She wasn't available to answer, so I left a voicemail.

"Hey, mom. I'm heading to Bristol now for an interview, so I'll be out for a few days. I'll try to keep in touch and update you on things. Bye now. Love you."

***

Daniel received me warmly and gave a listening ear to my story. He proved to be an amazing confidant and an unforgettable friend.

"Take all the time you need, girl," he patted my shoulder. "You can even take the bed; I won't mind sleeping on the floor."

"No, I won't. I said I wasn't going to inconvenience you, and I'm sticking to that. You've done enough by having me over already."

Nightfall came quickly and I couldn't sleep a wink. When the hour hand struck 5 a.m. I rose from the blanket on the ground and made for Daniel's bathroom where I bathed and dressed in readiness for the interview.

I was done in another thirty minutes and relocated to the living area with my documents. The wait for dawn was exhausting. Even when the day started to brighten up, I had to wait until office hours to visit. As soon as 7 a.m. came around, I said my bye to Daniel and took a cab to Emma's.

At the interview, Emma and I talked at length. She requested my ID, which I presented for examination. She ran background checks and handed it back to me.

"How'd you like to start with us on Monday?"

"Works for me."

"Good," she nodded. "About the pay, it's not much."

If only she knew that I was more than happy to work for a bar of Snickers.

"No problem," I replied, excitement bursting within me.

We concluded the meeting and I left for Daniel's. Immediately I touched down, I rang Mom. This time, she answered, and I told her about the new job. She was overjoyed. When my host returned, I told him the good news too. He congratulated me.

"So, what now?"

"I might have to stay here a little longer than I requested, until I can save up enough to get my own place. I know it's not what I bargained for over the phone, but you'd be doing me a real solid, Daniel."

"I get it. Like I said, take all the time you need."

"Thanks. You're a lifesaver. I promise not to inconvenience you or get between you and your flatmates."

He pulled me into a side hug and patted my back.

"Congrats again, Angie."

For another three months or so, I left for work from Daniel's and returned to sleep on his floor. Mom didn't know I was putting up with a guy, never mind sleeping on the cold, hard floor in winter. Even when I got round to finding my own pad, Daniel helped me out, giving me about £400 for the initial deposit.

And so, one phone call, a lie, and a location switch later, I'd gone from unemployed and borderline suicidal to a full-time gig and the company of the most amazing friend.

7

BLAST FROM THE PAST

A meagre wage for seven hours a day wasn't magical, especially as I only worked five days a week. It didn't help that I was brought in as a contractor and not a full-time worker—which cut me off from some benefits. My contract ran for six months, after which I'd be reviewed for a more permanent role. Basically, I'd signed up to be on probation.

But the nitty-gritty of my employment didn't dampen my happiness. The fact that I got to dress up in formal clothes and do what I loved was rewarding enough. I did my best for my employers until my contract ran out. During the final days, I applied for the position of payroll accountant in an accounting firm. With my CV now containing some formal experience, I was granted an interview, and consequently, the job. The timing couldn't have been better.

The position was priced at £17,000 per annum, which was a significant pay rise from my soon-to-be previous employment. I turned in my resignation and resumed at the new job, where I had a more defined position and benefits.

A week into my new job, I got a call from a multinational company I'd applied to during my exhaustive unemployment campaign.

It had been an exhausting day of balancing accounts and meetings at the office. I was commuting home when my phone buzzed. It wasn't my official number, so it couldn't be someone from work. I peered at the unknown number sprawled across the screen.

"Hi. Am I unto Angie?" It was a male voice.

"Hi. Yes, this is her."

"Right. So, I went through your CV—"

I blanked out at the mention of my CV. I'd only sent one of those since being employed. Even then, I'd sent out a gazillion before that time. I couldn't possibly remember where I applied to or when.

"You applied for the position of an assistant project manager."

It seemed more suspicious that I'd applied for a role I had no experience in. *How desperate did I get?*

"Hello? Are you still there?"

"Yes," I snapped out of my reverie. "Yes, please. Go on."

"All good. Did I catch you at a bad time? Do you have a moment to talk?"

"What? No!" I waved him off. "Please, proceed."

"Right. So, as usual, you're not the only one vying for this role, and I've spoken to everyone else but you..."

He seemed to trail off at some point and it took a moment before I checked to see if the call was still on. It was, but the reception bars on my phone had paled into the background, replaced by a poignant null.

I'd never experienced a network failure during my time in the UK. It made no sense.

"No. No. No…" I panicked, raising my phone high above my head.

Nothing.

"You've got to be kidding me!"

I rang the buzzer to alight and waited until the bus pulled into a shoulder. The call was still on, but static noises had replaced the rich, masculine voice on the other end. I pranced around the bus stop with my phone to the sky like a crazed influencer looking to start the next big challenge.

The tiniest bar crept into place, and I returned the phone to my ear.

"Are you still there?" his voice cackled and echoed.

"Yes. Yes. My goodness! I'm sorry. I might be having a bit of a poor connection. Could you ring me back in five minutes while I sort this out really quick?"

"Sure." he hung up.

I restarted my phone and waited for the cell towers to fall back into place. They didn't. I tried rebooting the device again when the call came in.

"Damn!"

I hit green. His voice flooded my ears in staccato symphony.

"Hello? I'm so sorry, but if you can hear me, can you try calling back in 10 minutes? I need to get out of this area in search of better reception."

He hung up again, and for the next 10 minutes, I scoured the area for good reception to no avail. The next time my phone rang, I didn't know how to proceed.

"Hey, Angie. Is it any better now?"

"Hardly. This is the first time I've ever experienced this."

"Right. Well, I don't think I'll be able to keep up with the poor reception. How about you come in for a face-to-face interview? I want to give you a similar opportunity to everyone else that applied for the position. This telephone interviewer just isn't doing it for me. Okay?"

"Very well, sir. Again, I'm very sorry."

"Good. I understand."

I sighed heavily, hearing the line go dead.

Onto the Next One

I got a link from the stranger, who had scheduled an appointment for three days later. Unlike my other interviews, I didn't prepare as much. In fact, all I could manage was to go through my previous CVs to get a refresher of how I'd sold myself to the company and the role they were hiring.

The interview was scheduled for Monday morning, and I couldn't afford to bail on my new job. I rang my boss, telling him that I'd be running late because of a doctor's appointment. With that out of the way, I proceeded to the address of the interview. The company was much larger than the one I worked for, with four times as many staff. It was interesting to see everyone in corporate clothes going about their businesses.

I was shown into the interview area and offered a glass of water.

"The interviewer will be with you shortly," the secretary smiled at me warmly.

"Thanks," I returned her smile.

She exited the room, leaving me to peruse the environment with my eyes.

"Hi, I'm Peter Williams. You must be Angie."

I rose to shake his hand, having missed his entrance into the room. His handshake was warm but firm, and he carried himself pragmatically.

"Please," he waved me to a seat across from him, getting down to business at once. "So, I went through your CV."

I nodded.

"Frankly, it's poor and unqualified. Truth be told, I've seen better CVs and more experienced candidates. But I want to give you the same opportunity as I gave everyone else that applied for the position. I was going to do it over the phone, but we know how that went."

"I'm sorry for your troubles, sir."

"Apology accepted. Shall we begin?"

"Please."

For about an hour or thereabouts, he quizzed me on behaviour and competence, taking notes as we talked. From his opening line about knowing better and more experienced candidates, I had no hopes of securing the position. Be that as it may, the questions were also not cheap. The bulk of them was completely over my head, and I had little idea of a few. But even with nothing to lose, I still gave my best shot in winging the answers.

The interview came to an end and Mr Williams put down his note and pen, stroking his temples.

"This went down much easier in my head," he chuckled.

You haven't the faintest clue, I smirked to myself. *Abu m nwa amara.*[88]

"I assumed it was going to be a straightforward process: you'll come in and I'll interview you. Then after a couple of days, I'd inform you that we can't take you. But after how you answered my questions and the warmth you exuded as you spoke—that gave me another think coming. I'm confused to say the least."

I offered a feeble smile.

---

[88] "I'm a child of grace."

"Well, I mustn't take any more of your time. I'll stew over it and let you know my decision in the coming days."

"Sure. Thank you for your time." I took his outstretched hand and saw myself out.

It wasn't until another four days that I heard from Mr Williams. This time, he rang me on his personal cell to ask about my availability for a second interview. I couldn't believe my ears. I hadn't given the job any thought since leaving the premises on Monday, and it was shocking to hear I'd made it to *second base*.

I agreed to the appointment and made arrangements with my current employer. This time, my excuse was another random appointment.

At the second interview, Mr Williams had brought some company from the board of directors: the Senior Project Accountant and the Technical Director.

My insides tingled as he made the introductions: the technical director managed one of the biggest portfolios in the country.

You've made it, babe! a smile danced on my lips, reflective of the excitement going on inside my head.

The interview ended as quickly as it began. Mr Williams didn't have any more questions, leaving the board members to indulge me the entire time. In the end, they excused themselves to talk privately.

"Hi, again, Angie." Mr Williams re-entered the room after some minutes. "We'll be making you an offer on the job."

My bowels churned, my heart rate doubled, and I found myself trembling with excitement.

"Oh! Thanks a lot, sir," I did my best to stay courteous, even though my head had gone agog with celebrations.

"So, the terms of salary: we'll be willing to pay £23,000 per annum."

The proposed amount was leaps and bounds above my present yearly salary, with the extra £6,000 sure to come in handy. I was going to agree to the offer when I had a gut feeling to test the limit they were willing to pay. Besides, I didn't know how tasking the gig would turn out. I was better off being adequately rewarded for my time and effort.

I made a face like I was pondering the amount and started in a solemn voice, "Sir, can we make that £24,000 per annum?"

"Yeah, sure. That's fine by us."

Dear God!

It was enough hard work trying to disguise the surprise at his response.

"So, when can you start?"

"I can start as soon as possible. I just have to turn in a notice to my present employers and stay out the waiting period. That should take about a week; I haven't been with them for long."

"Great!" Mr Williams withdrew his device and flipped through his calendar. "Would you be able to resume on 1 September, 2014?"

"Works for me."

"Very well, Angie. I look forward to working with you," he rose, fastening the button of his tux. "Have a good day," he offered his hand.

I took it, returning his smile. "Me too. Good day to you too."

As I left the premises, I couldn't contain my excitement. Within seven months, I'd gone from £5.35 wages to a £17,000 per annum gig to a £24,000 per annum role. I reached for my phone to call Daniel and my mom and broke the good news to them.

The prospect of working in a multinational corporation with a large and diverse workforce and a global presence was enthralling—the subject of wet dreams.

When I calmed down a bit, I realized the dilemma the new job had created. I'd only been at my second job for all of two weeks. Even more, my employers were nice, welcoming people, as were the rest of the staff.

How could I tell them I was moving on so quickly?

The next day, I called at my boss's office to tell him about the new appointment.

"It's a multinational company, and the position is in line with my credentials. Plus, it'd help me travel and I can still get a job with them even if I decide to live outside the UK. It's been beautiful working here and I feel a little odd bringing this up so soon. It's why I'm yet to accept their offer."

His face fell. "Well, don't make a hasty decision, Angie. Take your time. We're like family here, and you'll be sorely missed if you go. How about you take some days to think about it?"

"Sure," I nodded, saying my thanks and exiting his office.

My mind was already made up, but I waited out the notice period. My employers had been really sweet since applying, it was the least I could do to show my appreciation.

They were sad to see me go but understood that it was the best chance at achieving my goals. And so, on 1 September, I resumed my new job.

New House, New People

Mr Williams worked in the technical department, and I was on his team as an assistant project manager. He was the gaffer of major operations and a key player in the company.

From my first day on the job, he took me as his mentee. It was clear enough that he wanted me to excel at the role. However, regardless of his support, the first three months were a struggle. For the first time in my life, I had to put up with workplace bullying. There were a couple of people who found me an odd-fit and decided to bully me out of the position.

Competition was rife among some staff—and they were as toxic as they came. I wouldn't know how far my bullies could go until I was called in for a performance review by the end of the third month.

"I'm afraid your performance has been subpar," Mr Williams began, not taking his eyes off the file he was reading.

A knot formed in my chest.

"Some folks around her have come to me with negative reviews and whatnot. But I'm unconvinced, by both their sentiments and your performance. I think you can do better. Normally, with this sort of rating, you should be clearing out your desk as we speak. But I believe in you, Angie."

I felt myself breathe for the first time.

"Which is why I'm going to send you to a boot camp to sharpen your skills."

He dismissed me afterwards and I thanked him profusely. Returning to my spot, I pondered the bad egg that was trying to ruin my job, figuring it wasn't beyond Mr Williams' personal assistant. Now, that lady had had it in for me since I accepted the job. She was never nice to me and carried herself haughtily.

Mr Williams kept to his words and I was off to a five-day training camp in no time. The event was held outside Bristol, in one of the company's branches in Basingstoke. There, I met Frances, a lovely lady who took it upon herself to train me.

"I won't just train you, Angie. I'll help you live above those bullies and excel in your position," she said.

On returning, I was a different beast. I concentrated on work and blurred my bullies into the background. I grew into the role and thrived in it, so much so that my performances caught the eye of Mr Williams.

During a second performance review, he commented on my growth.

"I'm proud of you, Angie. Good job!" he smiled at me. "You know, you remind me of my wife: shy but capable."

Mr Williams' belief in me was enough motivation to do my best. Despite the negative reviews from my bullies, he turned a deaf ear and urged me on. I owe my success in the role to his mentorship and fatherly guidance.

Seven months after joining the company, I scored my first promotion. I was made the Assistant Project Manager to the National Grid—a position that involved managing the finances of the national grid. I wasn't as much a project manager as I was a commercial assistant and lead financial officer of all the portfolios on the national grid.

This new role elevated me to talking shop with the higher-ups, mainly technical directors, and sometimes, the clients themselves. It was mind-blowing the pace at which I was growing through the ranks, thanks to Mr Williams' interest in my success.

I began taking on larger and more important projects than before. Also, my bullies had become redundant thanks to the interests my new position had brought me. Other staff were becoming more receptive to me and everyone wanted me to mind their books and accounts. Now, everyone loved me and saw my hard work and efficiency.

The stone that the builders rejected had become the chief cornerstone.

By the year's mark, the company was bought over by another multinational corporation, and several positions opened up in the hierarchy. I saw an opportunity to go into the field I'd studied in university. Portfolio and project management was one thing, and accounting and finance in business was another.

The opening was for a project accountant for the Southwest portfolio. This position required relocating to a different office, which was still within Bristol, but outside the premises I'd worked in for the past year. Before applying for the job, I spoke to Mr Williams.

"Great!" he was encouraging. "It's about time you moved up the ladder, Angie. Go for it!"

With his backing, I applied for the position and got called for an internal interview and performance review. I was deemed fit and appointed for the role, which came with benefits of its own. For one, I was entitled to a salary increment.

As the project accountant, I was charged with overseeing over 400 project portfolios scattered across the country in places like Swindon, Plymouth, Bristol, among others within the Southwest. Also, since I was the only one managing the portfolio, I spent the bulk of the time travelling and growing my network. I met with several higher-ups in leadership positions, who loved my efficiency and approach to work.

After a year in the position, I was promoted to an even higher rank after my performance review turned out good. As a senior project accountant, I was entitled to a salary increment and newer benefits. My range also improved, and I could now meet with and talk shop with our London correspondents.

The End of an Era...?

Two years into my position as a senior project accountant, I decided it was time to leave and ply my trade elsewhere. I'd been with the company for years, so it made sense to me. I was still nursing the idea when the higher-ups caught a whiff of my plans.

One of my confidants must have slipped it to them, I imagined.

Never had I seen company leaders so adamant about leaving personnel. I was bombarded with calls and meetings, all geared towards making me change my mind.

"We can't afford to lose you, Angie," one of them had said on a call.

"But, sir, don't you think it's time for me to move on?"

"Why so soon? Are you unhappy with your role? You've only been here, what, two years?"

I chuckled. "It's been longer than that, sir."

"Nonsense, Angie! Anyhoo, you give me a week to come up with something. Until then, don't think about moving."

For the next couple of days, the executives lobbied to create an opening for me in the hierarchy. We weren't hiring at the time, and every position was filled. But they were determined to keep me at all costs. The result was to make me a financial controller, a new position with even higher pay and better benefits.

But it didn't end there. My portfolio was swapped, and I was given one of the high-profile projects in the United Kingdom that was valued at £1.1b. My company was the main contractor of the portfolio, courtesy of the new gaffer I'd be working under—an executive, Mr Ian Newiss, who called the shots on the project.

He had won the company the project, which brought in the highest revenue across the system. So, the company was always eager to appeal to him.

I had to switch offices again to be closer to the clients, who required full-time involvement. After the switch, my new boss invited me for a chat. We spent some minutes talking about me and my history in the organization.

"How much do I pay you, Angie?" he aberrated from the subject.

"Pardon?"

"How much do I pay you?"

You'd think that I'd be immune to such offers having begun my job at the company with a salary of my choosing. But I wasn't. I pondered the figure for a while and settled on one that wasn't greedy but sufficient enough to cover my needs.

"Sounds plausible," Mr Newiss nodded, pencilling down something on a notepad. "Anything else you'd like to add?"

I was dumbfounded for a bit but shook it off to answer his question.

"Well, I'd love to further my education. Get an MBA and all."

"That's thoughtful," he twirled the pencil before scribbling on the notepad again. "It can be arranged."

I doubted if he took my second request any seriously because he offered no objections or clauses. If the company was to ever sponsor my education, I'd have to do it their way, that's for sure.

Anyway, I put the thought behind me and settled into my new role. Mr Williams was ecstatic about my promotion and didn't cease to sing my praises to anyone who cared to listen.

At the time, he'd been made redundant and let go by the company. This development saddened me greatly, but he was quite wealthy and could manage without the job. He invited me for drinks with his staff to commemorate his send-off.

***

A year into the job, I was doing quite well for myself, even though the job was tasking. Added to the task of managing a huge portfolio, a collaboration with three other companies was subsequently added to my charge. The job brought me in contact with other fields in the industry, engineers especially, who I hung out with for so long I almost learned freehand sketching.

By the turn of the new year, I approached Mr Newiss for a discussion about my future.

"Hi, sir. Do you have a minute?"

"Sure, Angie. Please," he waved me to a seat. "What do you want to talk about?"

"It's about my MBA, sir. I think I'm ready to pursue it now."

"Right. That. Okay," he nodded. "You just have to apply for it now. I'll get in touch with the others."

Well, that was quicker than imagined.

I thanked him and left to write an application. All I had to do was convince the company how an MBA would help me, and why they should finance it.

Easy, right?

Well, the company rarely ever sponsored anyone in my position for masters. But my manager came through, helping me to secure the funds. In the end, they were willing to sponsor 80 percent of the charges, leaving me with the other 20 percent, which didn't amount to much.

Even after registering for an MBA, I still had to come to work. The company imagined I would sign up for a part-time programme, but I opted to go full-time. Knowing myself, I'd have easily tired of part-time studies, losing motivation until I gave up eventually.

Instead, I challenged myself to juggle full-time work and school. Unsurprisingly, it was the hardest I'd ever had to push myself. In fact, at some point, I couldn't attend lectures because work needed my attention more. Even when my schedule was balanced again, I struggled with both engagements.

A typical workday began at 7 a.m. and closed by 5–6 p.m., after which I headed for the library to study until 1 a.m. when I returned home. Some light, two- to four-hour sleep later, and I was back in the rat race. This was my routine from Mondays to Fridays. During weekends when I was off work, I spent the time buried in books and school work.

There were times when my schedules clashed and I had to skip work for some hours to attend an important lecture. During those moments, I reported to Mr Newiss and explained the situation to him. He was very supportive and gave me ample time to return to work. The cycle got tiring at some point, and I pondered ditching school.

After all, I'd done well without an MBA so far. What could it hurt?

But I couldn't bring myself to give up. Not now, at least. I'd successfully navigated the toughest periods in my life to come this far. *Why should this be any different?*

I'd gotten married during the start of my MBA, and coming home to do my fair share of spousal duties after a full day of work and school was doing my head in. Sometimes, I had dinner as late as 11 p.m.

It didn't help that my job was demanding in and of itself. Now, I had quotas to meet and financial turnovers to achieve, not just for my primary employers, but for the other companies in my portfolio too. On the school front, I spent some of my days in the library crying into my books. You'd think I was forced to learn. But my tears didn't stem from being compelled against my will.

I wanted to study and get my masters, but the stress was starting to get to me. I cried for release, and as a prayer for the strength to persevere until the end.

All my hard work paid off in the end: I graduated with a second class upper.

With my schedule freed up, I put more time into work, becoming more proficient, what with the new skills I learned at school. My colleagues were amazed by how I'd successfully rounded up my MBA in a year while holding down my position.

AFTERWORD

All's well that ends well.

Some two months after my MBA, a reputable government organization poached me, offering me the role of a lead cost comptroller. In retrospect, it seemed surreal that only a couple of years back, I was just another village girl with a blurry future.

Now, I'm being sought after by multinationals, have a masters in the bag, and a great man for a spouse. My husband, Ifeanyi, was a real sweetheart, supporting me at every turn and helping me scale obstacles. He didn't try to put me down or box me with expectations. We got married traditionally in 2018—I was 28 at the time. But it wasn't until October 2020 that we had a proper church ceremony.

If I had to choose, I'd pick Ifeanyi all over again. We are similar in many ways, from temperament to interests, among other things. He's made a name for himself as an engineer, and together, we've successfully bought a house of our own.

God has been faithful to us, and my faith in him couldn't be stronger. I want my story to inspire others: the broken, the wounded, and the disbeliever.

If only you can be patient and persevere. There's a time and a place for everyone. Believe in yourself and your craft and don't waver in your stance. Because when the wind of life turns and God's mercies come, you'll be transformed over and beyond your expectations.

I'm currently employed at a company I've always dreamed of working for, managing several projects within the public sector, including people who have been here for ages. Even better, I'm pursuing a PhD. What more could I ask for?

In retrospect, I could have wound up killing myself, giving up when I had to repeat primary school, or falling out when I couldn't get into secondary school. I've gone from lying on my resume to getting well-paid jobs and working with some of the most reputable professionals in the country. I went from being unable to string a good sentence in English to working with natives of the language.

Thank you for reading my story. I hope it brings you hope and helps you navigate the trials of life.

I look forward to updating you on the progress of my life going forward.

Ngozi Okoko

Page intentionally left blank

171

Page intentionally left blank

172

Page intentionally left blank

Printed in Great Britain
by Amazon